Lawrei
Halprin's
Skyline
Park

Lawrence Halprin's Skyline Park

Ann Komara

WITH A FOREWORD BY **Charles A. Birnbaum**
AND AN ESSAY BY **Laurie D. Olin**
EPILOGUE BY **Lawrence Halprin**

An initiative of The Cultural Landscape Foundation
Charles A. Birnbaum, series editor

Princeton Architectural Press, New York

Modern Landscapes
TRANSITION & TRANSFORMATION

The Cultural Landscape Foundation that focuses on historically important midcentury works that have undergone significant change. Each publication in the series chronicles the planning and design motivations behind the work, illuminates its history, places it within its historical design context, and, perhaps most importantly, draws attention to midcentury landscape treasures while raising awareness of their unique design value, inherent vulnerability, and historic preservation needs. Edited by Charles A. Birnbaum, the foundation's president, the series balances programmatic, design, historic preservation, and environmental concerns while providing a best-practices model. Depending on the landscape, this may include research and documentation efforts, design and treatment interventions, or ongoing management practices and strategies.

Published by
Princeton Architectural Press
37 East Seventh Street
New York, New York 10003

Visit our website at www.papress.com.

The Cultural Landscape Foundation

University of Colorado
Denver | Boulder
College of Architecture and Planning

Editor: Nicola Bednarek Brower
Designer: Elana Schlenker

Special thanks to: Bree Anne Apperley, Sara Bader, Janet Behning, Fannie Bushin, Megan Carey, Carina Cha, Andrea Chald, Russell Fernandez, Will Foster, Jan Haux, Diane Levinson, Jennifer Lippert, Jacob Moore, Gina Morrow, Katharine Myers, Margaret Rogalski, Dan Simon, Sara Stemen, Andrew Stepanian, Paul Wagner, and Joseph Weston of Princeton Architectural Press —Kevin C. Lippert, publisher

This publication was funded in part by a grant award from the State Historical Fund (SHF), a program of History Colorado, the Colorado Historical Society. The contents and opinions do not necessarily reflect the views or policies of the society nor does the mention of trade names or commercial products constitute an endorsement or recommendation by the SHF or the society.

Library of Congress Cataloging-in-Publication Data
Komara, Ann E.
Lawrence Halprin's Skyline Park / Ann Komara ; foreword by Charles Birnbaum with an epilogue by Lawrence Halprin. — 1st ed.
p. cm. — (Modern landscapes: transition and transformation)
Includes bibliographical references.
ISBN 978-1-61689-091-9 (pbk. : alk. paper)
1. Skyline Park (Denver, Colo.) 2. Parks—Colorado—Denver. 3. Natural history—Colorado—Denver.
4. Landscape architecture—Colorado—Denver.
5. Halprin, Lawrence. I. Title.
SB482.C6K66 2012
333.78'30978883—dc23

2012004969

Contents

Foreword

Charles A. Birnbaum

The role and value of landscape architects are becoming increasingly visible, particularly when they work on behalf of municipalities, community-based nonprofit organizations, and local stakeholders. As we have seen with the High Line in New York City (2009), designed by James Corner Field Operations and Diller Scofidio + Renfro, and more than three decades of work (beginning in 1980) by various landscape architects at New York's Central Park, their imprint and impact can be profound.

Yet, public interest in both stewardship and the transformation of designed landscapes is often lacking. If a historically significant or iconic building or its interiors are threatened with demolition or an unsympathetic alteration, there is often an outcry from the architecture community. Frequently, an informed debate plays out in the media, professional publications, and the blogosphere, and it is not unusual for boldfaced names, historic preservation professionals, the general public, and sometimes even the courts to weigh in. Watershed moments leading to this collective awareness include the demolition beginning in 1963 of New York City's Pennsylvania Station (which gave rise to massive national survey efforts and the national Standards for Rehabilitation and Guidelines for Rehabilitating Historic Buildings), and the subsequent proposed demolition of the city's glorious Grand Central Terminal, thwarted by Jacqueline Kennedy Onassis and other luminaries. More recent battles have been fought to preserve Edward Durell Stone's 1965 landmark of modernism, Huntington Hartford's Gallery of Modern Art at 2 Columbus Circle, and Gordon Bunshaft's (of Skidmore, Owings & Merrill) revolutionary 1954 Manufacturers Hanover Trust bank building at Fifth Avenue and Forty-Third Street (both in New York City). Today, when a building is at stake, architects, designers, writers, critics, artists, and even some politicians often band together, in pursuit of a solution that accommodates change through continuity. Whether the structure is ultimately rehabilitated or lost, one major result is that many are educated through the public vetting process.

Landscapes, on the other hand, often die quiet deaths, in part because the disciplines of landscape architecture and landscape preservation have, until recently, usually been at odds. The Modern Landscapes: Transition and Transformation books are a vital step in bridging that divide and raising the visibility of and understanding for landscape architecture and its practitioners.

An examination of Lawrence Halprin's Skyline Park in downtown Denver inaugurates the series. In this three-block linear park (designed in 1970, with the first block opened in 1973) Halprin employed nature as inspiration, interpreting Colorado's rugged beauty in a design composed of deeply recessed walkways that meandered through man-made steps and ledges. Signature fountains on each block, reminiscent of the region's red rock outcroppings, punctuated the scenographic experience. The park began as a huge success, but by the early 2000s, due to changes in use and adjacent construction, deterioration, a lack of programming, and poor maintenance, in addition to other social and physical problems, the park was perceived as uninviting. Prior to it being radically altered in 2003, university students with faculty supervision, empowered by a grant from the Colorado State Historical Fund, a program of History Colorado, documented the landscape to Historic American Landscapes Survey (HALS) standards. The project was the first such comprehensive research and inventory effort for a modernist designed landscape in the country and the first landscape documented in the state of Colorado (it bears the project number "HALS-CO-001"); much was learned about the park's design during the HALS process.

Lawrence Halprin's Skyline Park appears almost a decade after the original park's demise. The designer's intent in its creation and the process leading to its radical alteration can now be assessed. We can address whether the resulting forceful intervention was the best approach and, more importantly, how we measure success.

Introduction

**The essential purpose of design is to create
the possibilities for events to happen.
—Lawrence Halprin**

The city of Denver joined numerous other American cities in urban renewal efforts in the 1950s and 1960s conceived to revitalize and develop attractive downtowns. Denver's efforts included a thirty-six-block zone slated for demolition and rebuilding that became the Skyline Redevelopment Area. Skyline Park is centrally located within this area, occupying a one-hundred-foot-wide strip along the western street edge of three blocks of Arapahoe Street and straddling the Sixteenth Street Pedestrian Mall. [FIG. 1]

The idea for a downtown park surfaced in the 1950s among local business leaders, and a 1966 *Land Utilization and Marketability Study* restated this desire (see chapter 1). It first appears as a linear park lining the edge of three blocks along Arapahoe Street in a 1968 design sketch by Sasaki, Dawson, DeMay and Associates and Marvin Hatami.[1] In April 1970, the preeminent national landscape architecture firm Lawrence Halprin & Associates received the commission to design the park. Embracing the intentions of an earlier master plan for the area by Baume, Polivnick, Hatami, Halprin's team developed the design concept for the 3.2-acre linear park to reflect the local natural environment in a cool microclimatic contrast to the surrounding buildings and to create a hub, gathering places, and an exuberant urban promenade for Denver's citizens and visitors.

Halprin's impact on landscape architecture extends far beyond the strengths and influence of the projects that bear his name. While a critical appraisal of his legacy is still needed, it is possible to glean insights into his design process, his design expression, and the experiential aspects of his works by taking a closer look at one of his works—Skyline Park. Begun by Lawrence Halprin & Associates in 1970, the park went through two phases of construction, the first largely completed by 1973, with a final block and some additions completed in 1976. Sadly, Skyline Park was largely demolished in 2003 to accommodate a redesign sponsored by the city. The story of its conception, construction, and execution emphasizes the need to measure the impact and success of significant works of landscape architecture of the mid-twentieth century by understanding them not only at the time of construction, but also in the larger context of a collective cultural response since then. Skyline Park's demolition also points to the importance of developing frameworks and practices to preserve, rehabilitate, and interpret these works before they disappear or succumb to changing tastes or civic needs.

As seen in Skyline Park, midcentury landscape architecture can present idiosyncratic aspects—for instance, in experimental materials, spatial forms, or images. Some of these designs may not look like parks, but might read like pieces of sculpture, making it more difficult for contemporary audiences to appreciate or understand their value or contributions. For this reason, this publication posthumously analyzes Skyline Park, acknowledging both its position within Halprin's body of work and the qualities it brought Denver's renewal efforts. The book discusses Halprin's design of the park from concept through design development and construction. In explaining the park, it considers its physical elements and their role in creating an experience for visitors to the park. To offer ideas for those seeking to identify and preserve midcentury masterworks in their realms, the text concludes with observations on the areas of vulnerability and external forces to which Skyline Park succumbed and presents key pioneering documentation produced for HALS in May 2003, mere weeks before the park's demolition and subsequent redesign.

By the time Halprin was approached to design Skyline Park, his firm had gathered extensive experience in urban design, including streets, plazas, freeways, major movement systems, zoning

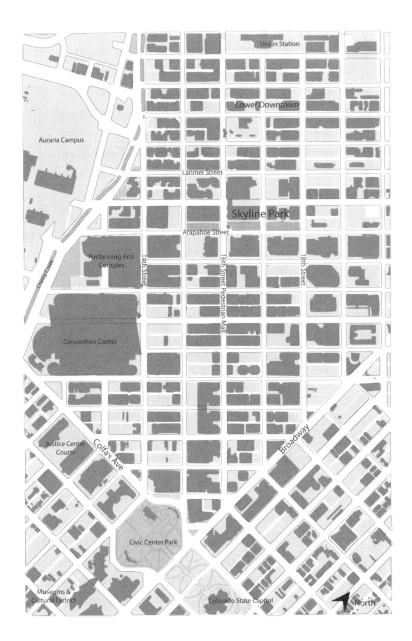

FIG. 1
Downtown Denver area plan
showing the current context
for Skyline Park with the
Sixteenth Street Mall and other
civic areas and buildings.

and development plans, and countless site-design projects. He had published *Cities* (1963) and had lectured and published broadly on urban issues. From his experience and travels he came to hold strong ideas about the potential for landscape in urban design, noting in *Urban Open Spaces* that "city is not so much a construction as a landscape of open spaces. It is a choreography of spaces, an ordering of movement through which we move and live our urban lives."[2] While there are many other designs that could be considered, a set of key urban works bear particular relevance to Skyline Park's conceptual and formal expressions and form part of its lineage and legacy within his body of work: Nicollet Mall, Minneapolis (1962); Portland (Oregon) Open Space Sequence (1965) [FIG. 3]; Seattle Freeway Park (1970); Charlottesville (Virginia) Mall (1973) [FIG. 2]; and Levi's Plaza, San Francisco (1978).

This collection of urban spaces, including Skyline Park, articulated some of the formal and experiential attributes inherent in Halprin's design approach, and reflected his attitudes about urban

FIG. 2
Halprin's work in other cities shows similarities to elements first expressed at Skyline Park, as seen in Charlottesville Mall's paving and pedestrian walks.

renewal. On a formal level, the two malls, Nicollet and Charlottesville, transformed urban streets into linear spatial structures through a series of spaces or moments threaded into a system of pedestrian movements that hold a linear directional flow regardless of where they are entered. On an experiential level, the Portland Open Space Sequence and Levi's Plaza exemplify Halprin's skill for designing places that celebrate nuanced experiences for visitors and gathering people into urban civic events. Skyline Park is in fact a convergence of these two realms. With its limited site running along three blocks, the park resembled the linear spatial pattern of the mall designs; the site response demanded a fluid movement that also enticed pedestrians to join the city's fabric at key points along the way. Since it was sectioned

FIG. 3
Resemblances with Skyline Park
are evident in Halprin's design
for Portland Open Space Sequence,
particularly in the block forms of
this fountain.

into three discrete parts by Denver's grid, the park also necessitated a design scheme that allowed people to gather and to find moments of respite and delight within a design that read as a whole. In response Halprin's office created a plan with distinct characters for each block, with three signature fountains and gathering spaces, that was in essence a condensed version of the Portland concept. Skyline Park is also similar to the firm's mall designs, however, joining its spaces in a masterfully choreographed sequence of pedestrian routes. The visitor's experience moving through the park sustained and forged connections between the blocks through a series of linked views connecting one part to the next. The design was further unified with consistent materials and planting, a hallmark of the Halprin office.

The park, a subtly orchestrated riff on the lessons of Nicollet Mall and the Portland Open Space Sequence, is thus firmly situated within the recognized canon of Halprin's urban works, a key

FIG. 4
Skyline Park looking eastward
from the Fifteenth Street entrance,
May 2003.

juncture in a set of design projects that sought to shape cogent, articulate frameworks for human experiences—places where people could connect to each other and to their environment.

Despite its pedigree, Skyline Park's role in the heart of Denver came under scrutiny and generated a decade of discussions and debate beginning in the mid-1990s. The park declined relatively slowly and was largely intact even in its last days. [FIG. 4] Its worn-out appearance and politics fueling debates about its future culminated in a call for its redesign. Initiated in 2003 the new Skyline Park design ultimately negated Halprin's vision, and the requisite demolition catalyzed the documentation effort behind this book. Reflecting upon Skyline Park's life, Mark Johnson, a preeminent local landscape architect, wrote:

> Regardless of the viability of the many modern landscapes in American cities, spaces such as Skyline Park were the embodiment of a high order of urbanistic thinking and ideals by the greatest talents of the time. The themes of city-building, healthy societies, and vibrant economies are embedded in the forms of these unique places. Whether they are worthy of preservation is a question that may take time to answer. They deserve, however, investigation, analysis, and judgment within their own time, our time, and that future time we cannot predict. When we look at the great cities of the world we always find layer upon layer of time represented in the urban landscape. Perhaps that is a clue about how we should preserve, modify, and rebuild these urban legacies.[3]

This book gives readers the opportunity to learn more about the life of Skyline Park, the history of its inception and its design, the uses it supported, and the memories it held.

1

Lawrence Halprin and Landscape Architecture

I felt this profession could combine everything I was deeply interested in: painting, design, botany, and community action.
—Lawrence Halprin, *A Life Spent Changing Places*

Lawrence Halprin (1916–2009)—landscape architect, ecologist, environmentalist, city planner, urban designer, traveler, writer, theorist, and artist—reveled in his work throughout a career that spanned sixty years, reaching nearly a decade into the twenty-first century. A prolific and nearly indefatigable practitioner, Halprin challenged the paradigms of landscape architecture through his extensive collection of built works and publications, as well as his social activism. He is noted especially for his emphasis on the design process and ecological principles, his sensitivity to human factors in design, and his investigation of movement and the experience of place. His obituary in the *New York Times* described him as "the tribal elder of American landscape architecture, who used the word choreography to describe his melding of modernism, nature, and movement in hundreds of projects."[1] Halprin's interest in cities and people generated a lifelong focus for his work. Tangible expression of these ideas is especially evident in his urban parks and plazas, including Skyline Park.

Now recognized as one of the most substantive and influential practitioners of the second half of the twentieth century, Halprin designed numerous projects, including the Sea Ranch (1962–65) on the coast of Sonoma County, Freeway Park (1970) in Seattle, the Open Space Sequence (1975) in Portland, Oregon, the landscape approach to the Falls in Yosemite National Park (completed in 2005), and many other public spaces. The Franklin Delano Roosevelt Memorial in Washington, D.C., begun with Halprin's submission to an invited competition in 1974, commissioned in 1976, and finally completed in 1997, is regarded as one of his finest projects and stands out in a body of work that ultimately has challenged the design profession to become more engaged with both people and our environment.[2]

Halprin's lifetime of achievement is reflected in a lengthy list of awards, citations, and honors.[3] [FIG. 5] A Fellow of the American Society of Landscape Architects (ASLA), he was awarded the most prestigious recognition by his profession, the ASLA Design Medal, as well as the American Institute of Architects (AIA) Gold Medal for Allied Professions and appointments to the first National Council on the Arts and first National Advisory Council on Historic Preservation. In 2003 President George W. Bush presented Halprin the National Medal of the Arts, the nation's highest honor for an artist. Ironically, these honors and awards placed Halprin at the pinnacle of his profession just as a number of his works were threatened with serious alterations or demolition, such as Skyline Park, where a full-scale redesign eradicated the integrity and substance of Halprin's plan.[4]

Halprin emerged as a leader in the practice in the decades following World War II, a period when landscape architects embraced new theories and areas for design, and designers across the board passionately pursued the era's social, environmental, and cultural agendas. He was at the forefront of expanding the landscape architect's professional scope to include new project types, such as office parks, plazas, corporate headquarters, airports, roof decks, and freeways. During this epoch, landscape architecture also embraced

FIG. 5:
Halprin's final office in Larkspur,
California, 2008. Note the
honors and medals displayed
behind his desk.

Selected Honors for Lawrence Halprin

Time Magazine Leaders of Tomorrow, 1953

AIA Gold Medal for Allied Professions, 1964

National Council on the Arts, 1966

National Advisory Council on Historic Preservation, 1967

ASLA Fellow, 1969

Institute of Interior Design Honorary Fellow, 1970

American Academy of Arts and Sciences, 1978

ASLA Gold Medal, 1978

ASLA Fellow, 1978

University of Virginia Thomas Jefferson Gold Medal in Architecture, 1979

Presidential Design Award, 2000

Bavarian Academy of Fine Arts Friedrich Ludwig von Sckell Golden Ring, 2002

National Endowment for the Arts Medal of Arts, 2002

ASLA Design Medal, 2003

Michaelangelo Award, 2005

large-scale regional and environmental planning, as well as urban planning and design. New professional foci arose to address industrial growth and development pressures, as well as the design needs of the rising middle class. Residential and suburban site planning and design responded to developing social behaviors related to leisure pursuits involving outdoor living, recreation parks, and greenways.

Urban theory and design became a major component of Halprin's practice and reflected his response to the rapid rise of the automobile, which facilitated a national exodus to the suburbs that resulted in the abandonment of city centers and subsequent urban renewal efforts, and a need for more sophisticated transportation and traffic planning. Halprin and other landscape architects addressed some of the challenges and opportunities Jane Jacobs identified in her seminal 1961 book *The Death and Life of Great American Cities*.[5] Halprin and Jacobs shared a fundamental belief in cities and their dynamic energy, and both understood the political underpinnings requisite to design change. Halprin's work affirmed his goal to make cities safer, livelier, and more diverse, filled with a variety of experiences and places.

Although some of the landscape designs produced in the postwar era maintained a traditional approach, a few key designers pushed practical or conceptual boundaries.[6] Several landscape architects explored spatial ideas drawn from film and the fine arts. Examples can been seen in Christopher Tunnard's awareness of a "space/time" experience when designing for the automobile; Garrett Eckbo's focus on transparency and layering in his work; and the influence of abstract art in projects by A. E. Bye and Geoffrey Jellicoe. Others, such as Halprin, developed design approaches that drew inspiration from fields ranging from ecology and sociology to the psychology of spaces and human interaction. Halprin was one of the earliest landscape practitioners to investigate the use of film or video to explore movement.[7] This medium allowed him to envision spatial and temporal relationships and was a direct outgrowth of his design training and his interests in human experience and an integrated design process.

In a 1992 article in *Landscape Architecture*, J. William Thompson provided perspective on Halprin's position in the history of landscape architecture:

> Halprin's work awaits a serious critical evaluation; yet, for many, his landscapes and urban designs constitute the greatest body of work by any 20th-century landscape architect. While his work is extraordinary in its range—it encompasses the suburban gardens of his early career, the exurban Sea Ranch and planning studies—its core canon addresses the re-animation of the center city. Like Olmsted before him, Lawrence Halprin succeeded in articulating a compelling social vision for the city. For Olmsted, the vision was one of pastoral relief from smoke and crowding; for Halprin, it was one of celebration of the city's rambunctious vitality.[8]

Scholarship on Halprin is evolving, yet much remains to be studied and written about his influence on twentieth-century landscape architecture. Of great value for this work is Halprin's final book, a memoir called *A Life Spent Changing Places*, published posthumously in 2011, two years after Halprin died after a brief illness at the age of ninety-three on October 25, 2009.[9] The following summary of his background, training, and design practice will set the stage for understanding Skyline Park as an example of his approach to the design of urban spaces and indeed of cities themselves.

Halprin was born on July 1, 1916, in Brooklyn, New York, the oldest child of Samuel W. and Rose Luria Halprin.[10] After attending Brooklyn Polytechnic Preparatory Country Day School from 1929 to 1933, he spent three years on an Israeli kibbutz, an experience to which he attributed his passion for collective ways of working.[11] He received his bachelor of science in plant sciences from Cornell

University in 1939 and his master of science in horticulture in 1941 from the University of Wisconsin.[12] Halprin later reflected, "At both institutions [I] put together an unusual assortment of courses—botany, geology, geography, landscaping—that transcended the norms of the time. I studied what amounted to ecology...but of course nobody called it that."[13]

While attending the University of Wisconsin, Halprin met his wife, fellow student Anna (Hannah) Schuman (born July 13, 1920), whom he married on September 19, 1940. [FIG. 6] They had two daughters, Daria (born in 1948) and Rana (born in 1952). [FIG. 7] Throughout their enduring marriage, Anna Halprin enjoyed a distinguished career as a pioneering modern dancer and choreographer.[14] Her work in avant-garde dance sought to break down or blur the barriers between performer and audience by removing dance from the theater and placing it outdoors, in the city streets and in nature. Halprin often collaborated with his wife on projects and workshops, and he credited her with developing his interest in exploring people's movements through space. An early article by Halprin published in the dance magazine *Impulse* lays forth some of his thinking: "Our gardens have become more dynamic and should be designed with the moving person in mind...a framework for movement. We are coming to realize that our everyday surroundings have tremendous importance in their influence on our emotional lives. The art process must be a total and continuing enterprise."[15]

The young couple moved to Boston, where Halprin entered the Harvard School of Design under a scholarship. At Harvard Halprin consciously expanded his already strong foundations with courses and research in architecture and urban planning, studying with many influential designers and theorists, including Christopher Tunnard, author of *Gardens in the Landscape* (1938), whom he regarded as the "most profound thinker on landscape architecture around at that time."[16] He was also inspired by architecture faculty members Walter Gropius and Marcel Breuer and their Bauhaus colleague, the Hungarian artist and furniture designer László Moholy-Nagy, who advocated the notion

FIG. 6:
Lawrence and Anna Halprin
as newlyweds during Halprin's
military training in Florida
before he shipped out on his
tour of duty, circa 1944.

FIG. 7:
Lawrence and Anna Halprin and
their young family, circa 1954.

that the arts were not disparate endeavors, but parts of one whole. Halprin came to believe in the collaborative predicates of "the Bauhaus… in Dessau [, which] had included dance, theater, costume, design." There were no pieces in the arts, he elaborated; they were "all one thing."[17]

From these mentors, Halprin learned that design and social issues do not exist as separate entities. He was also influenced by fellow students who would later achieve renown as architects, including Philip Johnson, Paul Rudolph, and Edward Larrabee Barnes. He developed a close friendship with William Wurster, a California architect studying at the Harvard School of Design, and they later collaborated on many design projects.[18]

In 1944 Halprin was commissioned in the U.S. Navy as a Lieutenant Junior Grade.[19] During a tour of duty in the Pacific his destroyer, the *USS Morris*, was hit in a kamikaze attack, resulting in hundreds of deaths. Sent to San Francisco on survivor's leave in 1945, he and Anna stayed in the Bay Area and developed their

FIG. 8:
Lawrence Halprin & Associates,
office photo by Jerry Bragsted, 1971.

interests in avant-garde art and design. Halprin began his career in
landscape architecture in the office of noted California landscape
architect Thomas D. Church (1902–1978), where he worked for four
years.[20] In 1949 he opened his own practice in San Francisco with
a handful of employees, including Jean Walton, a plant specialist,
who stayed with him for decades. Although much of this early practice focused on residential design, Halprin's strong environmental
and ecological thinking and his passion for social action remained at
the core of his interests. Soon the firm took on commercial and insti-
tutional design projects, in addition to housing and campus planning
work. Over the next decade, the number of commissions increased,
and new employees were hired; the firm took hold, becoming in 1960
Lawrence Halprin & Associates.[21] [FIG. 8]

Over time, Halprin's practice "attracted many of the best and the brightest designers from around the world who were intent on joining the high-energy…interdisciplinary group of planners, landscape architects, architects, ecologists, designers and photographers devoted to evolving experimental work that [addressed] broad issues of environmental design as well as social and political issues in regions, cities and public spaces."[22]

The firm's numerous design commissions gave Halprin the opportunity to develop and test his theories and ideas and refine his approach. In the 1960s he began publishing books about his thoughts and works, and he continued to study—often through sketching—the environment, places, and design concepts. In the first of his nine books, *Cities*, published in 1963 and revised in 1972, he wrote about urban form and movement:

> The city comes alive through movement and its rhythmic structure. The elements are no longer merely inanimate. They play a vital role, becoming modulators of activity juxtaposed with other moving objects. Within the spaces, movement flows, the paving and ramps become platforms for action, the street furniture is used, and the sculpture in the street is seen and enjoyed. And the whole city landscape comes alive through movement as a total environment for the creative process of living.[23]

Ghirardelli Square in San Francisco (opened in 1964), a collaboration with the San Francisco architecture firm of Wurster, Bernardi & Emmons, was an early project that carried out these ideas. It was "the first of the major center-city success stories to pair preservation with new economic uses," as Benjamin Forgey acknowledged in *Smithsonian* in 1988. "Halprin's contributions may have been the most important part of the puzzle—a site plan that takes advantage of San Francisco's slopes, and a sequence of buildings, stairwells, pathways and open spaces to keep every visitor happily moving."[24] The design creatively adapted historic structures; it also integrated underground parking facilities, a move echoed in other Halprin projects, such as Skyline Park.

  This innate respect for the site and emphasis on people's interactions and movements within it became Halprin trademarks and are consistently evident in his work. He honed his environmental awareness and sensibilities through observation and sketching during his many walks and journeys around California, throughout the United States, and abroad. Another important early project, the Sea Ranch master plan, encompassed five thousand acres along California's northern coastline. For Halprin it was "a breakthrough in basing a community's development on ecological principles and calling for as little intrusion as possible into the native environment."[25]

  During this period Halprin developed innovative conceptual approaches that emphasized the design process and participatory design: "motation," "scoring," and "the RSVP cycles," as he called them. Halprin conceived of motation, or movement notation, as "an alphabet of symbols indicating the principal characteristics of a given place and the speed and direction of movement through it."[26] He employed motation as a basic design tool, from which he could then, as he put it, "imagine how esthetic and human needs, such as skyline and other views, might be met in the design." Halprin's works emphasized movement to encourage interaction between the visitors and the space. "It is only when people are inside my design[s] and move through them that my design has any meaning," he wrote. "It is not what the design looks like that I am interested in; it is what it does [to] the people in it—how it interacts with them."[27] These ideas are very much in evidence in the development and resolution of projects such as the Portland Open Space Sequence, commissioned in 1961 and composed of Lovejoy Plaza and Pettigrove Park (both completed in 1967), the Auditorium Forecourt Fountain (opened in 1970), and the Ira Keller Fountain (1978); the Nicolett Pedestrian and Transit Mall in Minneapolis (opened in 1968, with subsequent additions);

Levi's Plaza in San Francisco (begun in 1978, dedicated in 1982); and Denver's Skyline Park (commissioned in 1970).[28]

As Halprin explains in *Cities*, his philosophy of fostering interactions between people and the city was a dynamic process imbued with opportunities:

> The provocative city results from many different kinds of interrelated activities where people have an opportunity to participate in elegant, carefully designed art and spontaneous, non-designed elements juxtaposed into what might be called a folk idiom, a series of unplanned relationships—a mixture of what is considered beautiful and what is considered ugly. These relations are often subtle and even disturbing. It is an environment which should provide those random and unforeseen opportunities, those chance occurrences, and happenings which are so vital to be aware of—the strange and the beautiful which no fixed, preconceived order can produce. A city is a complex series of events.[29]

For Halprin, creative opportunity was embedded within the context of the landscape. His emphasis on the processes of thinking and creating, grounded in his early affinity to ecological and human relationships, proved influential in the field of landscape architecture. His focus on the design process and the workshop approach that he developed legitimized these ideas and practices for other designers.

One of Halprin's earliest experiments revolving around the design process was a collaborative workshop that he and his wife conducted in 1966, which encouraged participants to explore and create an artistic experience. Building from this, Halprin soon began conducting public "Take Part" workshops in which constituents developed common goals for the design of community spaces. In *Process Architecture* he noted:

The way of going about things is as important to reveal as the
products themselves....You can view process as a way to arrive
at a solution, in which case it is a means toward an end, or you
can perceive it as important and valid in itself—full of twistings
and turnings, unknown explorations, reactive to many different
inputs and influences along the way, and lacking a clear image
of what the end product is or should be. What emerges then is,
in fact, "part of the process."[30]

Halprin was convinced that "people in communities could become
important influences on how those communities evolve." When used
effectively, Take Part workshops could lead to design solutions, such as
the Downtown Mall in Charlottesville, Virginia, which opened in 1976.[31]
          The Take Part approach led to Halprin's development of
"scoring," a graphic codification system of "processes which extend
over time"; the concept owed some of its origins to musical scores and
dance choreography, though in Halprin's version scores also showed
environmental aspects.[32] He adapted and used scores to record how
people create and to notate various parts of the design process and
visitor experience.
          The scores system is explained in Halprin's 1969 book
The RSVP Cycles: Processes in the Human Environment, which
offered an approach to design that allows for creative community
participation.[33] [FIG. 9] In this book Halprin states that a positive design
experience requires all four interconnected parts of the RSVP system
of Resources, Scores, Valuaction, and Performance. These cycles, as
Halprin explained, were a method for codifying and symbolizing ideas
in a common language for all participants, thereby enhancing their
comprehension of collective goals and the creative process. He wrote,

Working with the RSVP cycles [people] discover ways of
communicating with each other and arriving at creative
decisions based on multiple input. Then they can implement

Halprin's RSVP Cycle: Resources, Scores, Valuaction, Performance[34]

R: *Resources*, which are what you have to work with. These include human and physical resources and their motivation and aims.

S: *Scores*, which describe the process leading to the performance.

V: *Valuaction*, which analyzes the results of action and possible selectivity and decisions. The term *valuaction* is one coined to suggest the action-oriented aspects of *V* in the cycle.

P: *Performance*, which is the result of scores and the "style" of the process.

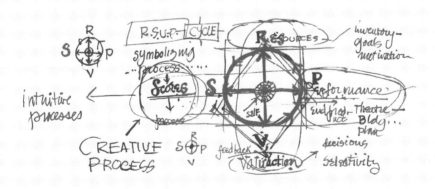

FIG.9:
Halprin's diagram of the RSVP cycles included notated comments regarding scores, goals, and other facets of the conceptual process and approach.

FIG. 10
View west through Skyline Park
from the Sixteenth Street Mall
toward the D & F Tower, May 2003.

what they want with the full support and enthusiasm of the
entire group. We hope to reveal things—what is the fundamental
human-environmental symbiosis…and how people can go
about providing it for themselves. It is a hope to design with its
inhabitants a human ecosystem biologically and emotionally
satisfying.[35]

Halprin believed that the built and natural environment critically
impacted the lives of everybody and that equal community participation, regardless of social, economic, and political status, was therefore fundamentally important to its design. He championed the
participatory process to address this need for social equity and also
to embrace change. As he noted in *Cities*:

Planners are beginning to realize, along with designers, that
their function is to guide change; not to develop static form or
fixed criteria, but evolving form. The search in our time is for
valid processes, and our urban forms will evolve and change
as part of our process of development and in response to the
changing technological discoveries of the future.[36]

Halprin's design principles and practices profoundly influenced
the work of his office, which continued to garner national recognition
for its work.

    No doubt Halprin's list of significant built projects, criti-
cal writings, and reputation helped the firm secure the commission
for Skyline Park in 1970. At that time Denver was seeking a strong
designer to execute the ideals of a master plan developed for an
urban renewal area that centered around a new park, and the city
hired Lawrence Halprin & Associates, by then a preeminent international presence in landscape architecture, to design it. [FIG. 10]

2

Conceiving the Park

You are what you live in....Cities don't have to be ugly.
—Lawrence Halprin

Denver's economy declined after the hardships of the Great Depression and World War II. By the mid-1950s, a swath of downtown blocks between Champa Street and the Platte River Valley and from Cherry Creek to Broadway showed the hard times. Tenants vacated buildings and maintenance lagged. Downtown emptied after business hours, and there was little in the way of activities or civic engagement. Formerly successful entertainment attractions, such as the theaters along Curtis Street, Denver's "Great White Way," lost patronage as newer and more elaborate movie houses and entertainment venues were developed outside of the city center.

In the heart of downtown, at the intersection of Sixteenth and Arapahoe streets, stood the Daniels & Fisher Department Store and Tower. When completed in May 1911, the tower stood seventy-two feet high and was Denver's tallest structure. Praised in local newspapers as "a monument by which Denver will be known" and

FIG. 11:
The future site of Skyline
Park, at the corner of Sixteenth
and Arapahoe streets, with
the abandoned D & F Building
and Tower shown in the late
1960s, surrounded by surface
parking lots and razed sites.

"a distinctive feature of a beautiful city," it also served as a beacon to draw customers to the five-story department store at its base.[1] "In 1957 the May Company acquired the Daniels & Fisher Company, and renamed all of its stores May D & F," noted Paul Foster in *Denver's Skyline Park—A History*, adding that the company subsequently consolidated operations, moving the May Department Store uptown to Sixteenth and Champa streets and leaving lower downtown without a major department store.[2] Exemplifying the urban decline, the old D & F Building and its iconic tower stood empty. [FIG. 11]

Civic Blight and Local Improvement Efforts

Acknowledging the gravity of the city's physical and economic condition, then mayor Will Nicholson created the Downtown Denver Improvement Association in 1954; its purpose was to meet with concerned business leaders to discuss the ongoing deterioration of lower downtown and its detrimental effect on the entire Central Business

District. In 1955 this group became the Urban Renewal Commission (URC) with the charge to address housing and urban improvements and "rid the city of blighted areas and slums…through rehabilitation and conservation of homes and neighborhoods in threatened areas."[3]

The members of the URC participated in meetings, conferences, and symposia about urban renewal and consulted with business and civic leaders from other cities in their efforts to find possible solutions for the urban malaise.[4] Resulting proposals ranged from mundane to futuristic, including an idea to build a mile-long Larimer Street Expressway.[5] The Centennial Plan of 1956 proposed multilevel underground parking and the relocation of city offices directly northwest of the former May Department Store site, soon simply known as the D & F site, with a new civic park spanning the blockwide and block-and-a-half-deep space north of the city office building.[6] Denver planners imagined that the private sector would develop new offices, hotels, and retail stores surrounding this civic complex. City officials expected the state and federal highway departments to finance the land acquisition and construction costs. However, when the timing proved too short to prepare for Denver's Centennial Celebration in 1959, this vision for a modern downtown failed to progress beyond initial planning.

In 1957 the Denver Planning Office and the URC produced a brief document called *Planning of the Central Area*, which included the first written proposal for a pedestrian mall on Sixteenth Street.[7] Like the 1956 plan it included a lower downtown expressway running through the Platte River Valley, and a new park site located near Lawrence and Fifteenth streets, a setting resonant for the location of the future Skyline Park. On March 10, 1958, the Denver City Council unanimously approved the reformation of the URC as the Downtown Urban Renewal Authority (DURA), a group that would be instrumental in directing planning for the future.[8] DURA worked closely with the Downtown Master Plan Committee, created to unite public and private interests around the common goals of strengthening the city's business appeal, tax base, and overall quality.[9] Together they generated development and funding strategies for a proposed urban renewal area named "Skyline," requesting federal funds from the U.S. Department of Housing and Urban Development (HUD) in 1964 to cover surveying and planning costs. Work on the Skyline Urban Renewal Project commenced under Thomas Currigan, mayor from 1964 to 1968, and reached completion under William H. McNichols, mayor from 1968 to 1983.

DURA: Skyline Park as a Catalyst for Urban Redevelopment

In 1965 DURA hired the Real Estate Research Corporation (RERC) to study the downtown renewal area. RERC formulated specific recommendations for the region, including proposing a public park to be developed at the site of the old D & F store.[10] The last park developed in the downtown area dated from the City Beautiful era at the turn of the nineteenth century when Mayor Robert Speer championed the Civic Center Park, which remains as the centerpiece of the urban parks connected by parkways developed at his initiative.[11] Downtown land subsequently became prohibitively expensive and was sold at such high premiums that creating a large-scale park had been considered too costly since then. However, RERC declared that an urban park was a necessary amenity if Denver was indeed planning for a city of the future. The report proposed that the D & F Building be demolished except for the tower to create a park that covered the entire block. DURA commissioners felt the real estate was too valuable for commercial purposes to devote the whole site to park space, so a more feasible proposal emerged featuring the venerable D & F Tower within a linear park three blocks long and a half block deep. This site became Skyline Park. [FIGS. 12, 13]

Natural disaster catalyzed the local planning effort. On June 16, 1965, major flooding of the South Platte River affected large swaths of lower downtown. This catastrophe, the worst recorded in Colorado in a century, spurred a reassessment of the urban plan and opened options for federal funding.[12] DURA and the Planning Office

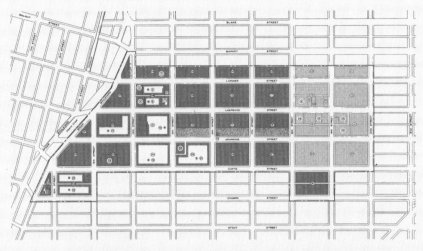

EXISTING DEVELOPMENT TO REMAIN ⊕
OR PROPOSED FOR REHABILITATION

(Refers to Circled numbers ①)
1. Larimer Square North
2. Laffite's
⊕ 3. Larimer Square South
4. Granite Hotel
5. Parking Lot
⊕ 6. Parking Lot (City)
⊕ 7. Parking Lot (C.B. & T.)
8. Tramway Power Plant
9. Dunn Shoe & Leather
10. United Distributing
11. Oliner's
12. M. L. Foss

13. Baker Electric
14. Isbell-Kent-Oakes
15. D & F Tower
⊕ 16. Central Bank & Trust
⊕ 17. Colorado University Denver Center
18. Frontier Hotel
⊕ 19. Brooks Towers
20. Cochran Building
⊕ 21. Federal Reserve Bank
⊕ 22. Police Block (City)
⊕ 23. City and County of Denver

MAP NO. 1 PROPOSED LAND USE PLAN
▓▓ General Commercial
▒▒ CBD Supporting Commercial and/or General Commercial
▨▨ Park
— — Project Boundary

SKYLINE URBAN RENEWAL PROJECT/COLO R-15

Denver Urban Renewal Authority
910 Sixteenth Street, Denver, Colo 80202   303/623-7114

FIG. 12:
DURA's Redevelopment Plan (1967) showing the Skyline Urban Renewal Project area with numbered blocks and proposed land uses, including the D & F Tower and what became Skyline Park along Arapahoe Street.

FIG. 13:
The aerial view shows the proposed blocks to be cleared for redevelopment, with the area slated for Skyline Park highlighted by the author to show its central position.

recognized that Denver's lower downtown area was fast deteriorating, and dramatic measures would be required to reverse the trend. In addition to advocating for necessary renovations of the infrastructure drainage system, they championed ideas for enhancing vehicle circulation and accommodating expansive new parking requirements. They commissioned local architects Baume, Polivnick, Hatami and their consultant Sasaki, Dawson, DeMay and Associates, a nationally recognized landscape architecture and planning firm from Boston, to produce a forward-thinking master plan for Denver's downtown.

The Skyline Master Plan

In 1967 that team presented the "concept, goals, principles, and standards to be carried out during the execution" of the Skyline Project, which it described as "a 37-block area of 157.7 acres located in the original core of urban Denver, but now referred to as 'lower downtown.'"[13] The report depicted Skyline Park as a formal, tree-lined linear promenade oriented along three blocks of Arapahoe Street, and also included criteria for adjacent building massing, an elevated

pedestrian circulation system, and underground parking facilities, all of which would subsequently shape Lawrence Halprin & Associates's design response. Interestingly, the newly appointed Denver Landmarks Preservation Commission and the Colorado Historical Society offered their endorsement of the Skyline project in 1967 through a resolution that stated in part, "Whereas the Historical Society has been assured that the final plans for the Skyline Project will include reasonable provisions for preserving and restoring important historic and architectural

FIG. 14:
"View of linear park and public plaza from elevated pedestrian way" by Baume, Polivnick, Hatami (1967).

structures within the development area and harmonizing them with the modern construction and open spaces involved."[14] Major preservation

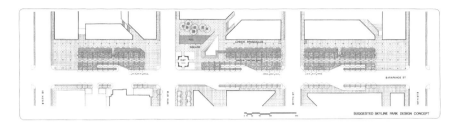

FIG. 15:
The Hatami and Tanaka team's design
concept for the park, March 1970.

efforts centered around the D & F Tower, though a few other structures within the renewal area also survived.

HUD authorized the Skyline project on February 27, 1968, in an agreement that "guaranteed U.S. approval, funding and working capital for the most comprehensive project ever undertaken in Denver,"[15] and DURA subsequently commissioned a follow-up study by Marvin Hatami, who was joined by Floyd Tanaka to prepare the new document.[16] Sasaki, Dawson, DeMay and Associates continued as landscape consultant, and Alan M. Voorhees & Associates of McLean, Virginia, served as traffic and parking consultant. The Hatami and Tanaka study continued to refine the concept of a three-block linear park, integrating this idea with an increasingly intricate fabric for the overall park design. Reflecting accepted practices of the era, a plaza connecting to street level and elevated pedestrian circulation routes were key components of the plan. The park linked the above-grade pedestrian circulation areas with the historic at-grade grid of downtown Denver. The D & F Tower became the park's focal point, with a large plaza surrounding the tower serving as the primary transition point to the elevated pedestrian areas.[17] [FIG. 14]

In addition to proposing the plaza at the D & F Tower, the plan suggested three other major grade-change transitions: one on the opposite side of Sixteenth Street, one near Fifteenth Street, and one near Eighteenth Street. [FIG. 15] The guidelines developed

FIG. 16:
Overhead view of a study model
showing Halprin's park design in
the area fronting the Park Central
Building at the corner of Arapahoe
and Sixteenth streets.

FIG. 17:
View of the study model along
the facade of the Park Central
Building into the park, showing
elements of Halprin's design.

by the design team for each block included
automobile access and egress ramps at three
locations along Arapahoe Street, which had
a major effect on the design of the park,
as reflected in the team's study and conclu-
sions for circulation and parking in the Skyline
Renewal Area.[18] These ramps, which would
be located at the park's perimeter, connecting Arapahoe Street to the
below-grade parking structure, were critical elements of the plan.

The master plan contained specific suggestions for the
design of the Skyline area as well as implementation standards and
criteria. The team carefully considered the design of the buildings
that would form the northwest edge of the park, especially at grade.
All of the buildings that joined the park's edge would be "compatible
in scale, height, bulk, and character with the civic scale and nature of
Skyline Park," and would be parallel with and extending no less than
80 percent of the entire length of Arapahoe Street.[19] Though some
minor variation would be allowed depending on which block was
being developed, these buildings were envisioned at least six and
not taller than twelve stories high. The drawings, plans, sections,
and perspectives suggested that the building facades at grade

should be developed as an arcade. This would provide shade and shelter for pedestrians, further enhancing the pedestrian scale and extending the depth of the park space.

Additional guidelines dealing with the D & F Tower block suggested that the park's northwest boundary should be extended approximately one-half block down Arapahoe Street to form a central design feature or gathering space. A large staircase at the northwest corner of this Tower Square was intended to forge the main connection to the upper plaza level, resulting in a smooth transition from the historic grid of the city to the pedestrian-only plaza. This block between Fifteenth and Sixteenth streets and Arapahoe and Lawrence streets eventually became the first block of the Skyline area to be developed in the Park Central Project. The plan suggested buildings of at least six and no more than ten stories to edge the park for a distance of at least 50 percent of the length of Arapahoe Street. Once again, the grade-level portion of the buildings was to be developed with a fifteen-foot-wide pedestrian arcade. At the corner of Fifteenth and Arapahoe streets, a building constructed on air rights over the parking garage would terminate at the park. The grade level of this structure was to be open, allowing pedestrians unrestricted movement.

The Park Central Building, initiated in January 1970, complied with the guidelines of the master plan. The Denver economy at that time was vibrant, and the developer chose a prominent local architect, William C. Muchow, founder of W. C. Muchow Associates Architects, with George Hoover as the project's lead designer. The Park Central Project offered great promise that the development of the Skyline area would indeed follow the Hatami and Tanaka plan with an at-grade arcade, pedestrian-scaled facades, plaza gateways, and pathways. Halprin, whose office was hired to design the park in 1970, collaborated with these architects as they worked out details for the first building bordering Skyline Park. Collaborative practices included sharing ideas, for instance by exchanging images of the models each team developed to explore their schemes. [FIGS. 16, 17]

3

The Master Plan: Connections and Infrastructure

We believe that existing cities are salvageable....
We believe that the future of human communities
lies in ecologically sound cities.
—Lawrence Halprin

The Skyline Park project came immediately on the heels of a critical period in the office of Lawrence Halprin & Associates. Between
1969 and 1970 the firm experienced a serious upheaval later
described in *Landscape Architecture* magazine as a "radical experiment in reorganization," a process that included an examination of
the firm's inner workings and management practices and challenged
the way Halprin engaged with both his staff and the design process employed.[1] In reflection, Halprin described it as a desire of the
younger staff "to rearrange what they considered to be a hierarchical
organization in which I controlled everything in the office....I faced
the difficult process of an intense reevaluation and restructuring of
my office. I found I was quite sympathetic with the need for change.
I was, however, opposed to a move toward chaos."[2]

The work on Skyline Park is representative of the firm's
design process from that period during which Halprin handed more

control over to the design team. In addition to Halprin, the Skyline Park team included firm principals Satoru Nishita, or Sat, who joined the firm in 1951, and Richard Vignolo, who started at the firm full-time in 1955.[3] Along with Senior Associate Jean Walton, these three had become, as Nilo Lindgren noted in 1973, "the principal partners, and the principal intuitive designers who backed up what Halprin referred to as his own flashiness."[4] Junji Shirai, a young staff designer in the firm, was also intimately involved in the project and is responsible for many of the design development drawings.[5]

Typical of the office's new working model, Halprin attended the start-up meetings and produced conceptual sketches, which he then handed over to the design team for development. He maintained design oversight and continued as the firm's figurehead and design arbiter, while Nishita wielded close control over the work done by the junior team member, with Vignolo occasionally weighing in, and also managing the project contract. Shirai's recollections of this time are insightful:

> Halprin assigned me to work on [Skyline] with Sat Nishita
> [, who was] head of design with me to support him. Halprin did
> not have much to say on the design direction except that he
> wanted to make it a predominant part of Colorado....Halprin
> occasionally came to my desk and gave me suggestions.[6]

This team and the time management practices in the office are indicated on the project's "Critical Path"—a wall-mounted visual flow chart denoting Skyline's deadlines and deliverables, personnel, and other details identified across time and listed in categories such as "job # and name, date/week, work, trip, cost, budget, date."[7] [FIG. 18]

This flow chart orchestrated the production of conceptual and schematic design studies and presentation drawings that led to design approvals and finally to the construction of the first block between Fifteenth and Sixteenth streets. Ideas that informed the development

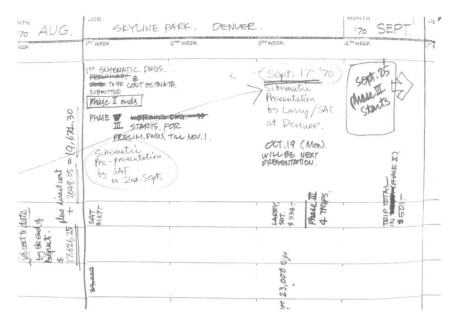

FIG. 18:
Detail of the Skyline Park Critical
Path, a visual road map for work
to be accomplished on the project
with notations for dates, deadlines
and presentations, personnel,
hours, and key deliverables.

of the final design included references to context and locale; dictates
or suggestions of the master plan; Halprin's ideas about urban design;
and specific site needs requiring technical solutions.

Influences: Reflect the Locale

Halprin and his staff studied local landforms and ecologies to create
a design for the park that would resonate with Denver residents and
visitors. Halprin's project notes and drawings reference the Colorado
foothills landscape. He was especially impressed with the sandstone rock formations typical of the Rocky Mountain foothills that he
explored on a visit to Red Rocks Amphitheatre west of Denver. His
interest in ecology and his sensitivity to patterns of water systems

prompted Halprin's particular notice of the foothill *arroyos*: deeply cut stream channels or canyons that support cooler, moister micro-climates with indigenous trees and shrubs. Characteristics of this landscape influenced the firm's selection of materials and colors for the park, as well as the layout and distribution of elements within the park's three blocks.

A key concept for the design was to create an *arroyo* atmosphere. The pedestrian experience was a sequence of spaces that alternately opened up and narrowed down. Each block offered a splashing fountain of water that in summer helped create a cool microclimate and served as a respite from the hot urban streets.

The material choices (see also chapter 4) referenced the coloration of Red Rocks's sandstone. As sandstone itself was deemed too expensive, concrete mixed with a local red sandstone aggregate was specified to simulate the stone. A tawny rose color tint was fully blended throughout, and the stone matrix was visible on all surfaces once they had been sandblasted, thus forging the local connection through color and also somewhat through texture. [FIG. 19]

The office considered another subtle reference to locale in design studies for the red brick pavers, which were based on Native American beadwork patterns.[8] The sketches show a series of alternative paving patterns, and the project design notes state, "Introduce Indian pattern on the brick pavement throughout from end to end. Regardless [of] the shape of pavement. Repeated continuous pattern."[9] [FIGS. 20–23] A chevron pattern was preferred, with the notation that it can "be seen from both directions," providing an interesting configuration regardless of the direction in which a visitor moved through the park. While this cultural reference was later abandoned, the studies highlight an attempt to find a local design idiom and point to the

FIG. 19:
Detail of the concrete matrix showing the integral red sandstone and tint of the concrete color. The sample was salvaged from the demolition in June 2003.

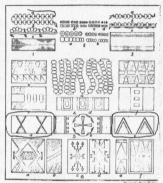

A

FIG. 20, top:
Research materials for paving from the Halprin archives show that the team studied this cut sheet from the Denver Art Museum files depicting Native American beadwork patterns for design ideas.

FIG. 21, middle:
Exploratory design studies inspired by Native American graphic patterns.

FIG. 22, bottom left:
This chevron paving pattern study, done in marker on trace, shows how the Native American patterns could be interpreted in bricks.

FIG. 23, bottom right:
Chevron paving pattern study as the designer developed it for walkways through the park. This sheet from the project notes also indicates the way the office worked: the team conducted research, undertook studies, which were usually discussed with Halprin, and then made a decision.

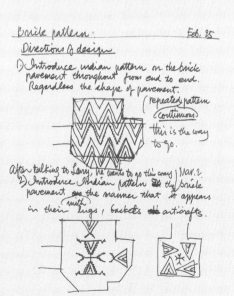

attention Halprin and his staff paid to both the design context and circulation system details.

Connections: Adherence to the Master Plan

With the master plan's template for developing the park site in mind, the Halprin design team studied the existing site conditions to address technical concerns and to develop the design of a dynamic urban space focused on the D & F Tower. This design ultimately shifted some emphases and details to conform to the team's own ideas, though much of the work adhered to the master plan's require-ments. Some of these requisites are noted in a March 1970 letter inviting Halprin to participate in interviews for the project. DURA Director Robert Cameron wrote:

> The design concept for the Skyline Project has been praised for its excellence and was recently given national recognition by a top design award presented by *Progressive Architecture* magazine. An outstanding feature of this concept is the separation of pedestrian and vehicular traffic by means of an elevated pedestrian plaza....Centrally located on these blocks will be the "gem" of the whole project, that is, the Skyline Park....The lineal configuration of the Park, coupled with the proposed adjacent development, encourages the design of the Park as an area of intimate human scale, visually and physically related to its surroundings. The landmark D & F Tower is to be retained and is envisioned as the focal point of the Park.[10]

The Halprin design addressed the master plan in several ways. First, the design strategy was based on the idea of an urban oasis—a distinct space engaged with but also separated from its surroundings. It would be isolated from city traffic and noise and meet the existing grades and proposed structural conditions, while also following the *arroyo* concept developed by the office. Key elements were a series of connections to

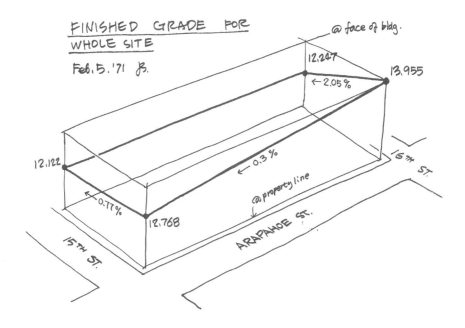

FINISHED GRADE FOR WHOLE SITE

Feb. 5. '71 JB.

@ face of bldg.

12.247

13.955

←2.05%

12.122

←0.3%

@ property line

16TH ST.

←0.77%

12.768

@ property line ↓

15TH ST.

ARAPAHOE ST.

FIG. 24:
A grading study by Shirai dated February 5, 1971, depicting the block between Fifteenth and Sixteenth streets. The study shows the necessary elevations to connect the park to its urban edges and gives a sense of the park's slight "tilt" or slope.

an elevated pedestrian circulation system and a fluid ground-level circulation system for moving through the park, a reflection of Halprin's motation concept. The designers also considered the massing and shape of adjacent buildings along the park's edge in an effort to create an appropriately scaled relationship and to avoid the feeling of a deep or dark canyon formed by tall, monolithic buildings. Walls and planter areas within the park created a distinct series of places that encouraged interactions among people. Finally, the park design addressed critical infrastructure needs for parking and urban drainage identified in the master plan.

Urban Oasis: Creating a Canyon in the City

Grading the park and shaping its interior spaces took place simultaneously. A grading study by Shirai [FIG. 24] shows desired connections to existing grade between the park and its surroundings, with corner

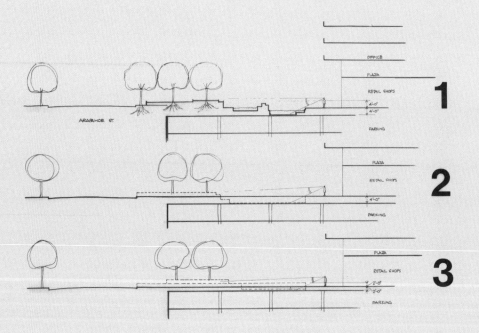

FIG. 25:
This untitled study depicting
sections and sight lines across
Block 18 demonstrates the visual
relationship of the site to the
street level and shows areas where
the water could be held. Felt
tip marker on pale yellow trace.

elevations indicating the gross pattern of slope and drainage for the initial construction between Fifteenth and Sixteenth streets. Two notated sketches in Halprin's hand identified elevations at the edges of the park and determined the relative overall change as it affected the design within the park.[11]

The relative overall change in grade across the site was no more than three and a half feet. By building up the park's edges along Arapahoe Street with berms, and by excavating down from the surface level, the interior park space was given a depth that added to its *arroyo* feeling. This approach to modulating space continued through all three blocks. As a design strategy, it enhanced the linear flow through the park, while maintaining fixed-grade relationships at the site's edges along Arapahoe Street as well as along the building fronts at the park's inner boundary. The grading was engineered carefully to support the park's function as a detention basin within the city's Central Business District drainage system. The walls and berms also buffered the park from the traffic, noise, and general hubbub of the street. Occasional gaps in the berms reconnected the visitor with the city. The internal spatial structure of the park used subtle shifts in elevation and changes in grade along the three blocks to create a dynamic experience for visitors. Halprin's conceptual studies also explored the visual implications for particular options by studying the relationships in elevation across the park from the Park Central Building (the first structure to be built in the first block) to Arapahoe Street, as figure 25 shows in three sections. [FIG. 25] The depth of the park's ground plane was not far below the street level, yet the sunken level created a feeling of enclosure and supported the larger master plan goal of managing stormwater collection and flow (see also page 60).

Pedestrian Circulation: Elevated Connections and Fluid Movement

Hatami and Tanaka's master plan strongly promoted the idea of elevated connections throughout a core area of downtown, reflecting popular urban design notions that had been tried with varying degrees of success in other cities, most notably Minneapolis. The plan "proposed a system of upper level pedestrian plazas [radiating from Skyline Park,] which interconnect all activities of the plaza area with all other commercial areas and Skyline Park."[12] This system was to extend throughout the Central Business District and create a linked sequence of lively open spaces and walkways removed from traffic.

W. C. Muchow Associates Architects provided a design response to this idea with its Park Central Building, located between Fifteenth and Sixteenth streets. A grand staircase leading from the heart of the Skyline fountain plaza to the building's second-floor entrance and terrace offered access to an upper-level pedestrian system that was to link into adjacent buildings and cross above streets.[13] The Park Central Building was the first built within the rede-velopment zone. The collaboration between Halprin's office and the architects and their engineering consultants led to a structure that fully engaged both the Central Business District's development design criteria and Halprin's conceptual ideas for Skyline Park. It was the only building developed adjacent to the park that addressed these concerns in this complete manner. [FIG. 26]

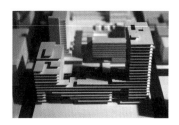

FIG. 26:
This museum board study model shows the massing concept for the Park Central Building and the elevation adjacent to the park site along the block between Fifteenth and Sixteenth streets (seen here as the flat space shown in the foreground of the model).

As Halprin's office approached the final phases of the project, it was part of a team that produced a series of design alterna-tives for the final block, located between Seventeenth and Eighteenth streets. These studies embraced the elevated pedestrian system concept, exploring a landing area in the park and the configuration for a bridge leading from Skyline Park over Arapahoe Street to the Mountain Bell Building, which was being designed by a local firm, Rogers/Nagel/Langhart Architects and Engineers.[14] One of numerous plans and sketches integrated the pedestrian-ramp landing into the easternmost block of the park. Despite the studies and serious consideration of the idea, neither the ramp nor the bridge were built, as ultimately cost and feasibility prevented any physical connection to the Mountain Bell Building. [FIG. 27]

Another architectural project for Skyline Park that embraced the idea of pedestrian bridges was the Tower Square collaboration with architects and developers Hensel Phelps, Van Schaack & Co., and Interface. The square was conceived as a new construction on the middle block, between Sixteenth and Seventeenth streets. Although it did not adhere to many ideals of the master plan, the team's proposal kept the D & F Tower intact and created a "complete separation of pedestrian and vehicular circulation via a readily accessible raised plaza and pedestrian bridges which link three perimeters of [the site] to the rest of the Skyline Urban Renewal Project. Sufficient commercial and entertainment activity is planned on this raised platform to make it a lively, vital segment of the city core."[15] Perhaps fortunately, this idea failed to gain traction, lacking approvals and funds, and the park space was left intact.

Massing: Creating Human-scaled Spaces

Early design sketches and notes demonstrate that the firm's goal was to acknowledge the master plan but also to design the park in a manner that infused the urban area with activity and functional spaces. A design note dated May 19 (1970) includes the following comments:

> If we cannot change any master plan given to us,—[arrow] We try to solve the problem of level crossing of ped.[estrians] at Seventeenth and Arapahoe in our site.—[arrow] We try to relate nicely to adjoining plaza levels, which are elevated about 1–2 stories high.—[arrow] We try to avoid a strong feeling of park being separated from major plazas by some means. Not this but perhaps like this.[16]

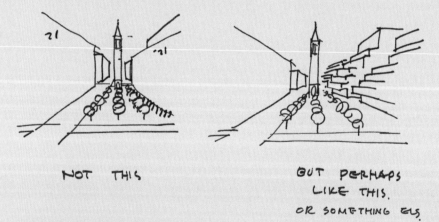

NOT THIS

BUT PERHAPS
LIKE THIS.
OR SOMETHING ELS.

FIG. 27:
This study by Lawrence Halprin &
Associates, January 22, 1972, shows
the landing and bridge that was
to connect the park to the elevated
pedestrian system proposed for
the Mountain Bell Building across
Arapahoe Street.

FIG. 28:
This sketch shows the massing
idea of a street that is not a chasm
of buildings but rather more open,
with buildings stepped back.

The accompanying sketch with stepped-back structures conveys the designer's idea to shape the pedestrian spaces and modulate the spatial massing in a way that allows air and light to create a sense of open space. [FIG. 28]

Gathering: The D & F Tower and Plaza

The most striking collection of early design studies focused on the D & F Tower, which had been identified as the focal point of the park. One note, from May 19 (1970), suggests an alternative in which the area around the tower contained a "tide fountain—which gives continuous rhythm to human life, and that on the weekend the program of water movement would be modulated to give more seating," and in winter "you can ice skate!" Within two weeks, the idea had shifted: "At the foot of the tower, the floor will be formed like steps. This canyon will be filled with water occasionally. When the open-air bazar [*sic*] (this will be a great tourist attraction) takes place, it will be dried up to give more interesting space for market place."[17] [FIGS. 29, 30]

Project design notes from June 5 (1970) suggest the precedents for the bazaar:

> Objectives of Flea Market (Sunday Bazaar)—is to stimulate minority groups' economic situation. Mexican, black, Indian's market where they sell their own products (handcrafts) or used household things. Just like other city's flea market (like Phoenix, Arizona, Cow Palace in s. S.F.) or "Olivera" at Los Angeles. Market Place will be owned and run by the City, and those who want to sell something have to pay $1.00 or $1.50 for fee per day, and one man can occupy no more than one bay or tent. Tent…supplied by city, will be colored so as to match the whole park area.—To give a human scale & feeling to the ultra modern office/residential downtown.[18]

FIG. 29:
Study showing the design idea
to activate the area around the
tower. Note that this alternative
assumed the closure of Sixteenth
Street, a decision that presaged
the Sixteenth Street Mall.

FIG. 30:
This study, which covers the
entire street space from building
edge to building edge, also
shows the intent to activate the
park's spaces with fountains.

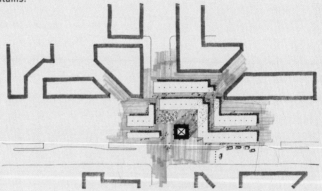

SUNDAY BAZAAR AT D & F TOWER SQUARE

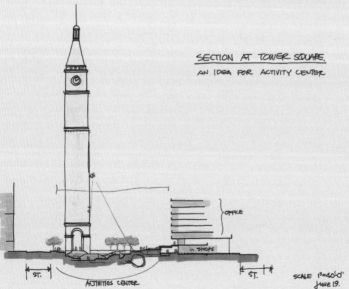

SECTION AT TOWER SQUARE.
AN IDEA FOR ACTIVITY CENTER

OFFICE

SHOPS

ST.

ST.

ACTIVITIES CENTER

SCALE 1"=40'0"
JUNE 19.

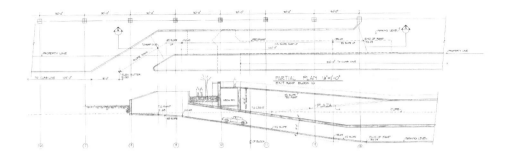

FIG. 31:
Partial plan and section of the
vehicular ramp to the parking
facility below grade in Block 18.

The firm's design for the park evolved over the next several months. Although the Sunday Bazaar idea was given up, the intent remained— the park should be active and lively, bringing people into the area, and the tower should be the enticement, the visual landmark to draw them in.

Infrastructure: Parking

When Halprin's office arrived on the scene, the Skyline Redevelopment Area presented a telltale sign of urban renewal: surface parking lots on sites cleared of buildings. In its bid to revitalize downtown, DURA sought to develop or support investments on these sites. To make this feasible, parking needed to be maintained during the construction of new buildings, and additional parking would need to be developed to serve new tenants. DURA and the Denver Planning Office therefore required development on the Skyline Park blocks to contain its own below-grade parking. When the park was built, this occurred below only the first two blocks, from Fifteenth to Seventeenth streets, with parking access and exit ramps onto Arapahoe Street. Halprin's office worked closely together with the architect and the consulting engineer, George Hadji of Los Angeles, to ensure their work would meet stringent requirements for bearing both live load and static weight from the park's infrastructure and landscape.[19] Confirming the importance of this are correspondence and drawings calculations, including, for example, a drawing that shows spot grades for the ramp and the planted park zone over the parking structure. [FIG. 31]

Infrastructure: Drainage Detention Basin

As part of the overall planning for downtown, DURA partnered with the city and county of Denver to address important issues related to flooding through drainage and detention measures. As noted by engineer Kenneth Wright:

> The archaic infrastructure and disjointed drainage policies in place in the six-county Denver metropolitan area during the 1960s left the growing area in a public health and safety predicament. In 1968, city, county, state, and federal engineers; lawyers; and politicians united to address and solve the core problems. Through the development of a comprehensive manual and the formation of a governmental entity responsible for drainage and flood control oversight of a five-county area, the seeds of a solution were sown. This endeavor required the cooperation and input of many experts, state legislation, public funding, and the genuine desire of all involved to work for "the common good."[20]

Skyline Park played a crucial role in addressing drainage and flood control. In correspondence with Nishita, George Hoover of W. C. Muchow Associates Architects noted that based on calculations by Hadji, "the park must be able to store water at a rate [of] two inches per hour to accommodate a rainfall rate of three inches per hour because DURA's water detention criteria permitted only one inch per hour to be let into the storm sewers." Hoover also noted that the park could detain a maximum volume of 6,680 cubic feet of water.[21] Halprin's team integrated these calculations into the park's details as the design development progressed. [FIGS. 32, 33]

FIG. 32:
Careful studies for drainage and details took place throughout the work on the project; one example is this study drawing from February 12, 1971.

FIG. 33:
A study sketch for an overflow drain inlet, dated April 1971.

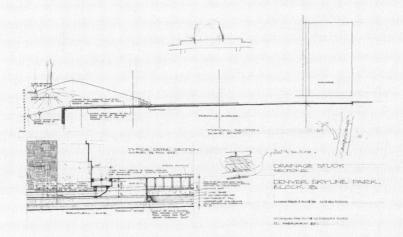

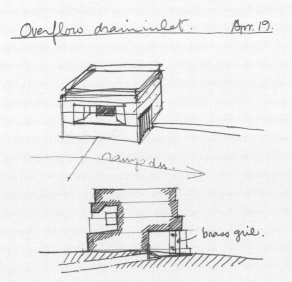

FIG. 34:
The drainage grate shown in situ,
visible at the left on the lower-
level area of the major gathering
space at the D & F Tower.

In 1997 the Denver Department of Urban Drainage
requested Wright Water Engineers to undertake a study of "the original detention criteria, the design of the Skyline Park drainage facilities, and the 'as constructed' facilities." Their findings showed that
the forty-thousand-square-foot area of Skyline Park would detain
24,930 gallons of surface water runoff during a ten-year storm at
one-inch depth, and during a one hundred–year storm would detain
a volume of 74,800 gallons at a three-inch depth.[22] This would essen-
tially prevent water from entering the parking garages below the park
and also slow any surge flows to nearby Cherry Creek, thus averting
any repetition of the disastrous flooding of 1965. [FIG. 34]

In a 1999 international symposium, Ben Urbonas, chief of
the master planning program for the Denver Urban Drainage and

Flood Control District, used Skyline Park as an exemplary model for urban stormwater runoff management, noting that Skyline was among the very few examples of detention facilities that "provide an aesthetic fit and a public function, such as parks, within the developments they serve." Skyline Park served as a detention basin within Denver's Central Business District and also as a plaza-park for the very dense commercial district. "During dry weather periods," he added, "it provides a pleasant environment for the shoppers, business people and workers to rest, walk, eat lunch, socialize."[23] The site engineering of this detention function placed Skyline Park at the forefront of the field as an integrated, aesthetically pleasing design solution worthy of emulation.[24]

      In retrospect it is clear that the park, thanks to the talents and insights of the designers in Halprin's office, successfully accomplished the objectives of the DURA Skyline Renewal Area master plan. A DURA document produced in the early 1980s to attract new investment and business to the area noted, "the future of Skyline/ Denver, the metropolitan area and the region are tightly linked. Once again, Denver's lower downtown is becoming a scene of exciting, bustling activity that is helping to influence and mold the future." The brochure stated that the park represented revitalization of "a significant portion of the central business district in a dynamic and growing metropolitan area...that serves as the commercial/financial 'hub' of a vast region where the Great Plains meet the Rocky Mountains."[25]

4

Materials:
Brick,
Concrete,
Trees

Skyline Park includes three major fountains designed
for a modern, unique and eye-catching appearance. Brick
and concrete walkways connect the fountains and wind
through grass-covered slopes dotted with trees and shrubs.
The entire park takes on a special appearance at night
when the fountains, seating areas and walkways are lighted.
—DURA, *Skyline/Denver*

The above description, published by DURA in a handsome promotional brochure, captures the essence of what Halprin's office was trying to achieve: a dramatic yet simple modern design for an urban oasis serving as a counterpoint to the skyscraper canyons of downtown. As we have seen, the firm carefully considered the site and program of the park in its design. Thoughtful material selections and designs for site elements, such as walls, paving, stairs, and furnishings, further refined the project. Planting reinforced the sculptural and spatial qualities of the park and softened the definitive lines of the concrete and brick. Three fountains (discussed in chapter 5) served as focal points, infusing each block with individual character. As this chapter explores, and as pages 124–25 illustrate, Halprin conceived the park's walls and cast-in-place concrete work; its site elements and fixtures, such as benches, drinking fountains, and lighting; and the plantings as an integrated vision and a unified whole. [FIG. 35]

Walking Surfaces: Brick and Textured Concrete

The materials and construction techniques were consistent throughout the three blocks of the park, although construction took place
in distinct phases, beginning with the block between Fifteenth and
Sixteenth streets, followed by the second, central block that included

the D & F Tower, located between Sixteenth
and Seventeenth streets. The last phase,
a separate contract with DURA, was the
block between Seventeenth and Eighteenth
streets, completed in 1976. The design team
employed a restrained palette of soft rust and
red tones for the brick and concrete surfaces.
The color of the pavers, which were produced
from local clay, provided a consistent reference to Colorado's red foothills.[1] The brick
pavers appeared in various gathering places,
such as the small plaza below the D & F Tower.
Even more direct was the use of local red
sandstone aggregate in the concrete mix used

FIG. 35:
To create the signage along the
Fifteenth Street flank of the block,
the park's name was formed directly
into the wet concrete of the wall
using Helvetica, a popular typeface
choice for Lawrence Halprin &
Associates, whose own letterhead
and title block were set in Helvetica.
This sign remains in situ.

for walkways, which was tinted a rosy hue that
echoed the local landscape, as seen earlier in figure 19. The firm's
design specifications directed where the exposed aggregate concrete
should incorporate Red Devil sand and where it should use Red Devil
three-quarter-inch gravel from a quarry in Colorado Springs.[2]

Concrete: Cast-in-place Walls and Other Elements

The extensive use of concrete for paving, retaining walls, seat walls,
and other features provided coherence across the three blocks.
[FIGS. 36, 37] The exposed concrete surfaces were sandblasted to
reveal to a greater or lesser degree the integral aggregate of the concrete mix. Walking surfaces were the most heavily sandblasted to
create a rougher texture to prevent slipping, while seating surfaces
were lightly sandblasted for a more comfortable seating surface. This

FIG. 36:
Concrete cast in place requires
careful preparation, evident
in the construction details for
a stepped retaining wall. This
section shows the six-inch band
and the one-inch step back
typical of the walls in the park.

FIG. 37:
Plan indicating the layout of
the forms that were used to cast
the wall. Specifications further
explained this process and the
desired surface finish.

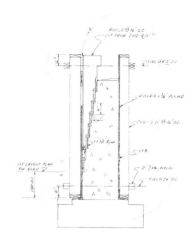

SECTION THRU WALL FORM

MAX RATE OF POUR 4'0' PER HOUR

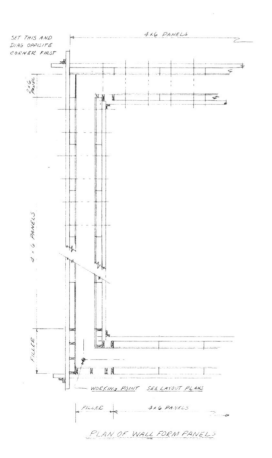

PLAN OF WALL FORM PANELS

FIG. 38:
The cast-in-place concrete retaining wall that created the berm along Arapahoe Street included stepped seating and stair risers, here seen at the western end of the first block, near the entrance at Fifteenth Street (May 2003).

FIG. 39:
Cast-in-place concrete walls, stairs, and seating lined the berm along the length of the park, starting at the western end near Fifteenth Street, seen here. This view also shows a built-in light fixture and one of the drain inlets at the pavement level (May 2003).

FIG. 40:
Layering the walls and narrowing the pedestrian space created a channeled experience, seen here in a portion running between the D & F Tower plaza and the fountain near the Seventeenth Street entrance to the park (May 2003).

FIG. 41:
Cast-in-place seating and fountain levels on the third block, near the entrance at the corner of Arapahoe and Eighteenth streets (May 2003).

distinction in the finishing displays the sophistication in design detailing and skill of execution typical for the Halprin office.

The signature detail repeated throughout the park was a pattern of six-inch-high horizontal bands. Cast in place on site, typically as walls, these bands were set back one inch as they rose in height above each lower band, as shown in the construction details in figures 35 and 36. The six-inch dimension was also used consistently as a measurement standard for stairs and other concrete features and elements within the park, resulting in a unified system of dimensions and patterns. The vertical bands created a striated visual appearance running across the park's vertical surfaces, such as retaining walls and the low edges of planters. The banded layers also appeared in stepped seating areas and lined pedestrian paths. [FIGS. 38–41]

Fixtures and Furnishings

The park's fixtures and site furnishings, including seating and benches, drinking fountains, and lights, were part of its general design vocabulary

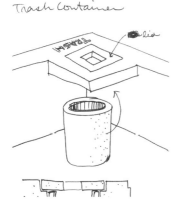

FIG 42:
Study sketch of a trash
container inserted directly into
the concrete wall system.

and were detailed in the firm's construction drawings. From the 1970s onwards, the Denver Department of Parks and Recreation added standard-issue trash receptacles, green metal signs, and lighting, all of which diminished Halprin's overarching design vision and intent.

Elements designed as integral components of the concrete wall system showed the attention to built-in detailing of functional features within the park. Trash receptacles, for example, were built into walls with their lids flush to the surface of the wall, as indicated in the design study in figure 42. The receptacles, however, did not function as planned, and were sealed and inoperative by the early 1990s. [FIG. 42]

Rather than using a prefabricated freestanding model of drinking fountain, Halprin's office chose simple, stainless steel basins with a single bubbler fixture manufactured by Haws Corporation of Berkeley, California, and integrated these drinking fountain units as part of the park's cast-in-place concrete columns or walls.[3] The sketch of the detail seen in figure 43 shows how the unit was to be built-in at an appropriate height, with the plumbing hidden within the wall, while the photographs in figures 44 and 45 reveal two different instances with the handsome basin set into its concrete shelf. [FIGS. 43-45]

Benches were also designed as part of the wall system, notably in the first block, in a seating area slightly removed from the pedestrian flow. Two sketches for this bench show the designers' attention to proportion and seating comfort. They also indicate how Halprin's team took accepted design standards—for instance, proportions or height of seat—and flexed them to adapt to the bench's particular site and material. This bench was attached to the concrete retaining wall with metal flanges and planked with wood slats, blending into the overall fabric of the park. [FIGS. 46-48]

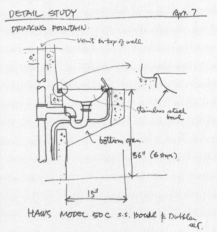

DETAIL STUDY   Apr. 7

DRINKING FOUNTAIN.

Vent to top of wall

stainless steel bowl

bottom open.

36" (6 steps)

15"

HAWS MODEL 50 C s.s. bowl & Dubler set.

FIG. 43, top right:
This study sketch for the
drinking fountain also reflects
the firm's depth of development
for details, and again emphasizes
the idea of integrating the
functional elements into the
concrete framework of the park.

FIG. 44, top left:
Haws drinking fountain basin
and bubbler integrated into a cast-
in-place concrete wall, shown
in situ in a front view (May 2003).

FIG. 45, bottom:
Haws drinking fountain, seen
in profile as it projects from
a cast-in-place layered retaining
wall (May 2003).

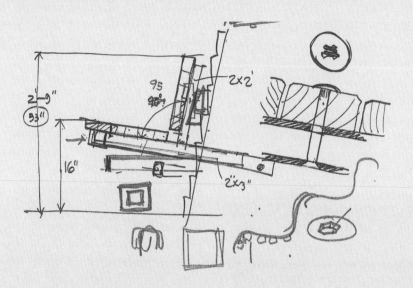

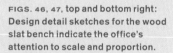

FIGS. 46, 47, top and bottom right:
Design detail sketches for the wood
slat bench indicate the office's
attention to scale and proportion.

FIG. 48, bottom left:
One of the park's benches shown
in situ attached to the retaining
wall of a low planting bed in the
middle of the first block, just east
of the fountain (May 2003).

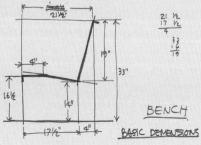

Lighting fixtures appeared throughout the park, enlivening the spaces and the fountains at night. The firm's lighting studies for Skyline Park include a blueprint of the drafted plan for the first block, with study trace taped over it containing notations for lighting. Prepared by Shirai, this plan, dated January 12, 1971, included areas keyed out for "higher intensity lighting [done with] horizontal flood-lights; low intensity [levels of lighting]; relatively darker areas; [a] special lighting area (fountain); [and an area that] needs co-operation with Muchow."[4] To accomplish this variation in the quality of the lighting, the team developed a typical palette of lighting elements. Characteristic of the firm's overall approach to functional details in the park, the design team integrated many lights into the concrete seat and flank walls of various ramps, stairs, and passages, such as those seen in figures 49 and 50. Tall, freestanding cast-in-concrete light standards lit the pavements throughout the three blocks, but they were most prominent in the final block, as seen in figures 50 and 51. [FIGS.49–51]

Planting: Sequence and Punctuation

Lawrence Halprin & Associates's planting plan for Skyline Park emphasized framed spaces and views, and supported the design intention of creating a pedestrian-scaled, cool microclimate foil to the surrounding city. The design used trees and fountains to establish an ambiance and signature character for each block. Although the planting layout patterns varied to reflect a conceptual idea of moving through different spaces, the choice of plants provided overall consistency with limited variety in notable spots. [FIG. 52]

A series of studies explored variations in the arrangement of trees for the first block near the corner of Sixteenth and Arapahoe streets. A conceptual idea that was carried through in the planting of all blocks was to use visually distinctive trees, such as flowering crabapples (*Malus species*), to mark park entrances, and to plant evergreen trees, such as spruce or pine (*Picea pungens glauca* or

FIG. 49:
Another view of the recessed
lights along the entrance ramp
and stairs coming off of Arapahoe
Street. Note also the drinking
fountain on the light column, the
tall light, and a drain at the lower
right of the image (May 2003).

FIG. 50:
Recessed lights along an
entrance ramp and stairs leading
down from Arapahoe Street
between Seventeenth and
Eighteenth streets (May 2003).

FIG. 51:
This view of the final block,
looking toward Eighteenth Street,
shows cast-in-place lights that are
recessed into the retaining wall
and a tall light standard constructed
atop the juncture of the seat and
retaining walls (May 2003). The
trash visible in this image reflects
the decline in maintenance that
started before the 2003 demolition
was confirmed.

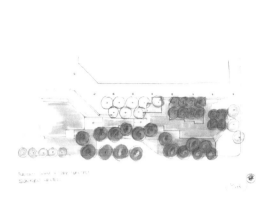

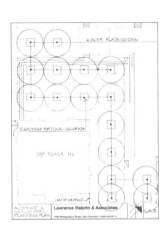

FIG. 52:
Schematic study for planting, showing the area in front of the Park Central Building closest to Sixteenth Street.

FIG. 53:
This planting plan study, "Alternative A," shows a tightly organized arrangement of deciduous trees to frame and set off the base of the D & F Tower.

Pinus nigra), to maintain visual interest during the winter. Several design development sketches also considered the spacing and selection of plant species. One alternative for planting at the base of the D & F Tower shows a grid of maple trees (*Acer platanoides*) and underplanting of the locally hardy groundcover, wintercreeper (*Euonymus fortunei colorata*). [FIG. 53]

These studies culminated in a planting plan for each block. Honeylocusts (*Gledetsia triacanthos inermis*) planted along the Arapahoe Street edge linked the park's three blocks, and a consistent and restrained palette of plants was used across the whole park. Each block had some areas of grass, shaded areas of seating, and plants marking entry points, as seen in the planting plan shown in figure 53. In the first block planting was relegated to the edge berm and a few planters, due to constraints of load bearing over the parking garage below. Planting in the middle block was more open, with trees framing the pedestrian walks and gathering spaces. The third block was the most heavily planted with trees, offering a contemplative shady grove. [FIG. 54] The dappled shade and beauty of this block made a pleasant counterpoint to the busy urban context.

The major tree species used for the block between Seventeenth and Eighteenth streets reflect the palette used throughout the park:

Street trees:
Honeylocust *Gleditsia triacanthos inermis*

Shade trees:
Green Ash *Fraxinous pennsylvanica lanceolata*
Norway Maple *Acer platanoides*
Red Oak *Quercus borealis/rubra*

Ornamental trees:
Crabapple *Malus species*
Japanese Maple *Acer ginnala*
Ornamental Plum *Prunus species*

Coniferous trees:
Austrian Pine *Pinus nigra*
Colorado Blue Spruce *Picea pungens/glauca*

Over the years the plantings became the least intact aspect
of the park, reflecting both maintenance neglect and the decline that
is part of the natural process of plant life cycles. An analysis of the
planting design in 2003, shortly before the park was demolished,
shows the difference between the park's condition then versus the
original planting plan.[5] Plants were located on berms along Arapahoe
Street, in large concrete planter boxes, or, in the D & F Tower area,
in tree pits surmounted by tree grilles installed flush with the pedestrian surface. Many areas that originally had been planted with grass
or groundcover were barren patches of earth, which the city of
Denver had covered with a layer of shredded bark-fiber wood mulch,
in layers about three inches thick.

Trees were overgrown, missing, or in a few instances, left as
stumps. The tree palette, although significantly diminished, remained
much the same as in the original plan—a limited list that reflected
the systematic use of deciduous street trees along Arapahoe Street,
deciduous shade trees and ornamental trees for visual and seasonal
interest throughout the park, and ornamental and evergreen trees to
mark entrances.

The restrained material palette used throughout the park—
from consistent planting and the line of street trees to concrete
coloration and treatment, from custom lights to trash receptacles—
allowed the design to read as a connected and unified whole spanning three blocks. It was not a traditional, pastoral park; it was an
experience of place, a choreographed sequence of spaces in a sculp-
tured landscape. Halprin's signature use of water in the park's three
fountains, discussed in the next chapter, added the final touch to the
design and provided each block with a unique character within this
cohesive linear whole.

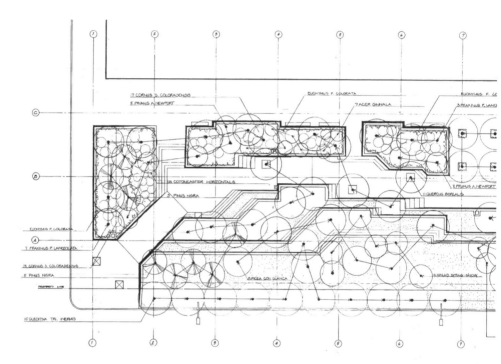

FIG. 54:
Planting plan, Block 16 (between
Seventeenth and Eighteenth
streets), dated September 2, 1975.
Lawrence Halprin & Associates,
for the city and county of Denver.

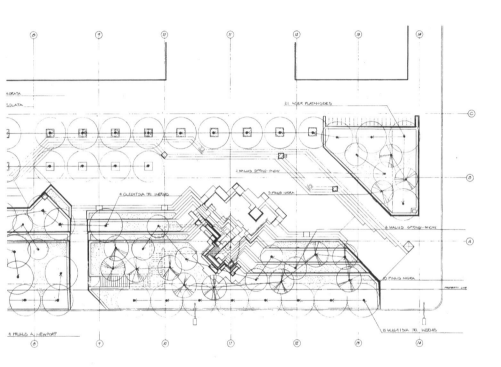

PLANT LIST AND LEGEND

TREES

QUANTITY	BOTANICAL NAME	COMMON NAME	CALIPER	HEIGHT	SPREAD	BRANCH CLEARANCE	DESCRIPTION	ROOT
21	ACER PLATANOIDES 'EMERALD QUEEN'	NORWAY MAPLE	4"-4½"	15-20'	10'-12'	6'-7'	MATCHED	B&B
7	ACER GINNALA	AMUR MAPLE	2"-2½"	8'-10'	6'-8'	LOW	MULTISTEM	B&B
11	PRUNUS AMERICAN NEWPORT	PURPLE PLUM	3"-3½"	10'-12'	6'-8'	3'-4'	FULL BRANCHED	B&B
11	QUERCUS BOREALIS	RED OAK	3"-3½"	12-15'	6'-8'	6'-7'	FULL BRANCHED	B&B

GROUND COVER

AS NEEDED	EUONYMUS FORTUNEI COLORATA	PURPLE LEAF WINTERCREEPER			8"OC		MIN 3-4 STEMS 9-12"	3"POTS

PLANT LIST AND LEGEND

TREES

QUANTITY	BOTANICAL NAME	COMMON NAME	CALIPER	HEIGHT	SPREAD	BRANCH CLEARANCE	DESCRIPTION	ROOT
10	FRAXINUS PENNSYLVANICA LANCEOLATA 'MARSHALL SEEDLESS GREEN ASH'	ASH	4"-4½"	18-20'	10'-12'	4'-5'	FULL BRANCHED	B&B
27	GLEDITSIA TRI INERMIS 'SKYLINE'	HONEY LOCUST	4"-4½"	18-20'	10'-12'	6'-7'	FULL BRANCHED	B&B
14	MALUS SPRING-SNOW	FLOWERING CRABAPPLE	3'-4'	10'-12'	8'-10'	3'-4'	FULL BRANCHED	B&B
8	PICEA CONCOLOR GLAUCA	COLO. BLUE SPRUCE	3'-4'	10'-12'	10'-12'	3'-4'	FULL BRANCHED	B&B
21	PINUS NIGRA	AUSTRIAN PINE		10'-12'	6'-8'	3'-4'	FULL BRANCHED	B&B

SHRUBS

45	CORNUS STOLONIFERA COLORADENSIS	RED TWIG DOGWOOD			5'OC		3'-4'	B&B
10	COTONEASTER HORIZONTALIS	ROCK COTONEASTER			4'OC		18-24"	B&B

SOD	EQUIVALENT TO 93% IMPROVED VARIETY MERION BLUE (LESS THAN 1% WEED CONTENT) NOT LESS THAN 1" THICK, OR APPROVED EQUAL.

5

Water:
The Signature
Fountains

Water reminds us of high mountains and streams, of deep chasms and gurgling brooks and the quiet sounds of the wilderness. Even in a city, the sound and sight of water stirs the most elemental and basic roots of our human natures.
—Lawrence Halprin, *Cities*

Water was a dominant visual and experiential aspect in many of Halprin's urban designs. Fountains played an important role in notable Halprin projects in San Francisco, Portland, and Seattle, as well as the FDR Memorial in Washington, D.C. Halprin understood water's essential human appeal. His lifetime collection of sketchbooks revealed his ongoing fascination with its qualities and properties. He drew it in myriad forms and circumstances: ocean waves over rocks, stream flows and eddies, urban fountains, water in pools, jet sprays, and droplets. [FIG. 55] It is no surprise, then, that water features prominently in signature fountains in each of Skyline Park's three blocks. Though sited individually to activate specific points of interaction with visitors, the fountains linked the linear park sections as consistent, expressive elements. Halprin championed the idea that water and sculpture belonged together, noting in *Cities* that "the abstract qualities of the sculpture and the movement of water are interlaced into a complex composition."[1]

At Skyline Park, the first block, between Fifteenth and Sixteenth streets, contained a freestanding fountain that invited exploration with its water sheeting over high sides and collecting in a raised concrete basin surrounding the sculptural forms. The second block featured a fountain close to Seventeenth Street, drawing people into the park. Balancing the dominance of the D & F Tower at Sixteenth Street, this fountain was composed of a series of cubic blocks arranged in a composition of varying heights with water bubbling out of the top and dropping into lower blocks and layers of pools. The third fountain was located near the northeastern corner of the park at the Eighteenth Street entrance. Anchoring the northern end of the third block, this fountain featured cascading tiers of water rippling over shallow ledges and surfaces into small pools. [FIG. 56]

The fountains forged a connected set of landscape features that punctuated and dominated a visitor's experience of the park. Conceptually, they reflected the landscape of Denver's foothills and their *arroyos*, where streams cascade over red sandstone rock into deep channels. The transformation and abstraction of this design inspiration resulted in these inviting, powerful visual features whose cascading waters muffled traffic and created a microclimate of cool relief from the urban heat. This was the essence of Halprin's fundamental ideal of connecting people with nature through water. In *Cities* he noted, "There is a quality about water which calls to the most deep rooted and atavistic part of our nature. In the deep canyons of cities, water, along with fire, trees, and the almost hidden sky above, are the elements which can still tie us to our primitive past."[2] In Skyline Park the fountains created a lively ambiance and offered visitors opportunities to explore, play, and get their feet wet in this realm of urban nature.

Skyline's First Fountain

Although conceived as a set, each fountain reflected variations in design and construction, and each fountain's mechanical pump and water systems functioned independently. The first fountain, demolished

FIG. 55:
Halprin's sketch of the Pacific
shore near the Sea Ranch captures
his interpretation of water's
direction, flow, energy, and rhythm.

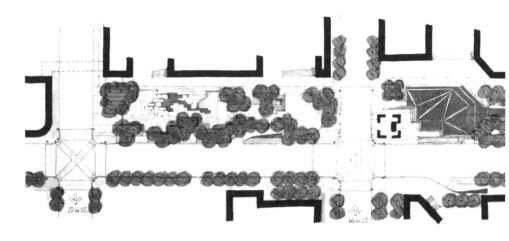

SCHEMATIC PLAN

BLK. 18 WATER FALL

Aug. 17

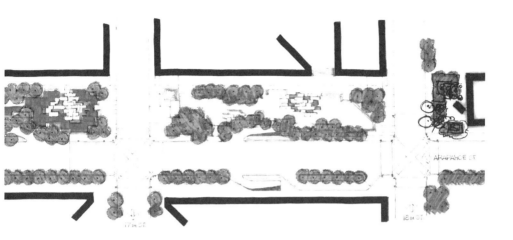

Lawrence Halprin & Associates

1620 Montgomery Street, San Francisco, California 94111

FIG. 56:
An early presentation drawing
for the city and county of
Denver and DURA, dated August
28, 1970, shows Skyline Park
with fountains located in each
block and a ribbon of trees planted
across all three blocks. Drawn
at a scale of one inch equaling
forty feet, it was rendered in
markers on a blackline print of
the park's base plan.

FIG. 57:
This study was part of a set of
five alternative design concept
studies that explored variations
for fountains and active public
spaces for this area of the first
block; this version showed an
elaborate water wall and elevated
connection promenade to the
proposed Park Central Building.

during the renovation, was located midblock between Fifteenth and Sixteenth streets in front of a flight of stairs leading up into the Park Central Building. Early conceptual studies by Halprin's team included elaborate integrations of fountain and architecture, such as walkways and a viewing promenade on the second level leading into the building.

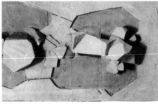

[FIG. 57] These early studies generated the basis for the fountain's location, which maintained its central position within the block. During design development the team explored many iterations to determine the fountain's scale, fit, and form in drawings and models, such as the clay model seen in figure 58, which shows the fountain within the context of the block and the proposed adjacent building. [FIGS. 58, 59]

Once its location was settled, the fountain still required numerous studies. Originally, the designers hoped to fabricate this first fountain from large blocks of local Colorado stone arranged to simulate a mountain cascade. This proved untenable, however, due to structural weight limitations related to the parking levels below. In seeking a solution that would achieve the design intent and still meet load restrictions, Lawrence Halprin & Associates brought in consultants and investigated other, more feasible material options and fabrication alternatives. [FIGS. 60, 61]

Working closely with Halprin, Nishita and Shirai collaborated with Los Angeles sculptor Herb Goldman (born in 1922) to design this first fountain. They also engaged the fountain consultant Richard (Dick) Chaix of Beamer Wilkinson, who specialized in hydromechanics.[3] Halprin formed a close working relationship with Chaix,

FIG. 58:
The office used clay models such as this one to study the fountain's massing and relationships, in this case with and without the stepped setback, and also to explore the design alongside the proposed Park Central Building.

FIG. 59:
This photograph of the clay study model for the fountain was one in a series that explored the shadows cast by the fountain. The water basin at the base of the sculptural form was tinted with blue marker to indicate water.

DENVER SKYLINE PARK BLOCK 18
FOUNTAIN STUDY
SKETCH FROM 3/16 PRELIM. CLAY MODEL.

LAWRENCE HALPRIN & ASSOCIATES
LANDSCAPE ARCHITECTS
1620 Montgomery Street
San Francisco, California 9411

1st JUNE 71.

FIG. 60:
A pencil sketch from June 1971 was drawn from the 3/16-inch preliminary clay model to convey the fountain's form, shape, and surface.

FIG. 61:
Partial frontal view of the first fountain with the Park Central Building in the background. Taken prior to the fountain's demolition in 2003, this photo captures the water's character, flowing for the final time.

and they would continue to work together on numerous projects, including Freeway Park in Seattle and Levi's Plaza in San Francisco.

The design team eventually settled on using Gunite, a sand and concrete mix sprayed at high pressure through a hose over steel or mesh form, to create the fountain. This cost-saving and weight-reducing measure accommodated the complex sculptural shape. Perhaps more important, the fountain was basically hollow, built of structural steel and mesh faced with only six inches of applied, tinted concrete. The final product was therefore much lighter than solid concrete or stone, a factor critical to realizing this focal landscape feature while respecting the block's stringent weight restrictions for structural load. With Gunite sprayed to a thickness of six inches, the fountain, whose shape covered about 3,776 square feet of surface, encompassed 1,888 cubic feet of sprayed concrete mix.[4] To fabricate it, a shape was first built of steel and mesh. Mechanisms and pumps necessary for producing the dramatic water display that enticed visitors to walk around and through the fountain were located inside the fountain and in a small mechanical room nearby. [FIGS. 62, 63]

FIG. 62:
Fountain interior with steel mesh frame, bracing, and part of the recirculating water pipe.

FIG. 63:
Fountain interior with steel mesh frame with part of the recirculating water pipe and pump mechanism.

Halprin's idea of creating an interactive fountain appeared consistently throughout the design studies, though the form varied as the constraints shifted the design solution. The study in figure 64 captures this well, showing the early formal vocabulary considered for this first fountain. [FIG. 64] Although the stacked-block shapes did not appear in the final version for this block, the idea was retained, informing the fountain designs in the next two blocks.

<u>Water area for block 18.</u>   Sept. 4

Some ideas: ---

1. Using same system as steps around depressed area ....

→ walk through

2. Completely different from surrounding area. but! keeping ~~sys~~ simple module system.
(any kind of shape)

→ walk through.

FIG. 64:
This early study by Shirai shows the idea of a path leading through the fountain and hints at the final composition, although the fountain forms became more organic and less blocky.

FIG. 65:
DURA Skyline promotional material, with a caption that read: "An eye-pleasing feature of Park Central is the Denver Urban Renewal Authority's Skyline Park—an environment of lush grass, stately trees, red brick walking paths, contemporary rock formations set off by a series of sparkling waterfalls. Fuller and Company is proud to be a part of DURA's unique park setting."

Skyline Park

FIG. 66:
This view eastward from the
D & F Tower shows the second block
between the Sixteenth Street Mall
and Seventeenth Street, with the
plaza below the tower, the parking
egress at the center right, and
the blocky forms of the fountain.

As installation progressed, one Denver observer remarked that the fountain was "designed to resemble piles of red rocks up to twelve and a half feet high with waterfalls and water cascades. Three sets of steps are to lead to the top of the fountain and three passageways are to enable persons to walk through the fountain and under the waterfall."[5] The result was enormously successful, building support for the park and the renewal area. [FIG. 65]

The Second Fountain

The design for the park's middle block, containing the D& F Tower, balanced this iconic historic structure with a strongly defined fountain centered within the width of the park at the opposite end of the block. [FIG. 66]

This fountain, another collaboration between Chaix and Halprin's design team, closely reflects Shirai's original sketches, with strong rectangular volumes, stacked and arranged to allow exploration within, through, and around the fountain. Emanating from basins atop several of the cubic shapes, water flows over the edges to the pool at the base below the plaza level. The firm's design studies for this second fountain were just as extensive and no less detailed than for the first. Early sketches, such as those shown in figures 67 and 68, reiterate the cubic shapes but also show a general concept for the water's flow and patterning and, with steps and multiple levels, hint at the idea of accommodating people. [FIGS. 67, 68]

Fitting the fountain into its setting while accommodating human interaction drove much of the design development, with

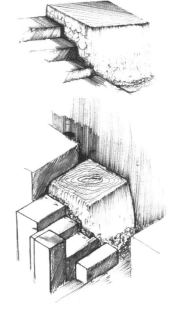

FIG. 67:
Envisioning the steps in another view, and possibly for another part of the fountain, this study captures the quality of the water as it spills over the edge of the block.

FIG. 68:
Design study, ink on trace, for the second fountain, with steps indicating the intent to invite people to interact with the fountain.

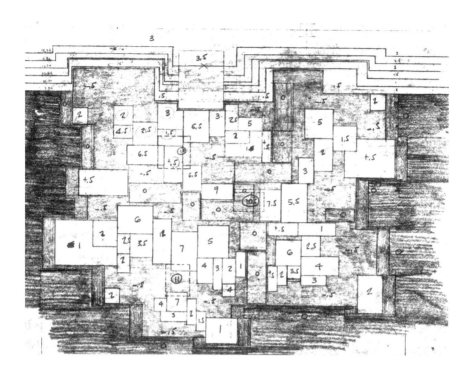

FIG. 69:

This study of relative heights
for the block units reveals Shirai's
methodical approach to the
scale and shape of this fountain.
As this plan shows, he set an
imaginary elevation "zero" as
a datum, roughly corresponding
to the base level for meeting the
adjacent grade. He then recorded
the relative height up or down
from that. For instance, a "5"
means that block is five feet above
the zero base line. Changes in
the block heights are shown
in half-foot units, and the darker
area is the basin or catch pool
for the water that flows from the
three areas noted in the sketch.

some of the most interesting studies for
this fountain exploring the stacking, relative heights, and arrangement of the block
shapes, as seen in figure 69. This drawing,
one of several that wrestled with this idea,
shows the designer reconciling the heights
of the blocks in increments related to each
other. [FIG. 69]

Further studies refined the scale
and proportion of the fountain, ensuring that
it would be visually balanced and engaging.
A set of drawings, including the study in figure 70, explored through
section and elevation the relative size of the fountain, which was
adjusted to fit the site and human proportions. [FIGS. 70–73]

FIG. 70:
This study, done in ink and
pencil on yellow trace, translated
the plan drawing into a frontal
view showing the relationship
of the massing of the fountain
blocks to a human scale.

FIG. 71:
Perspective sketches such
as this one capture the human
scale of the fountain in relation
to the large blocks, animated
with water moving over them.

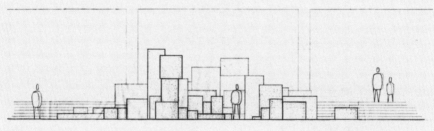

SKYLINE PARK, BLK 17,
SOUTH EL. FOUNTAIN, 1/8"=1'-0"
L. HALPRIN & ASSOC. June 20, '72

DENVER SKYLINE BLK 17
FOUNTAIN   June 20'72
Lawrence Halprin & Associates
1620 Montgomery Street San Francisco California 94111

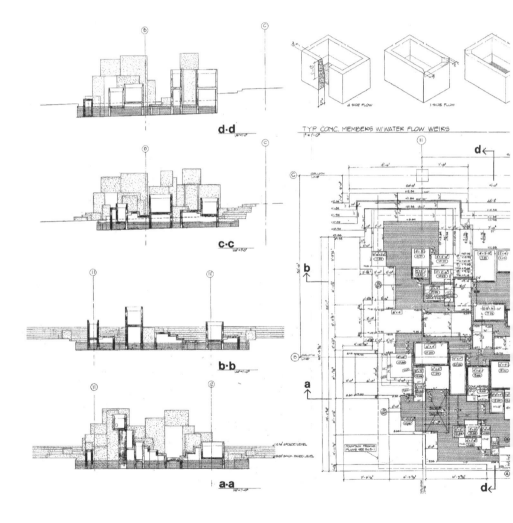

FIG. 72:
Layout and details for installing
the cast-in-place concrete
fountain are included on this
construction drawing.

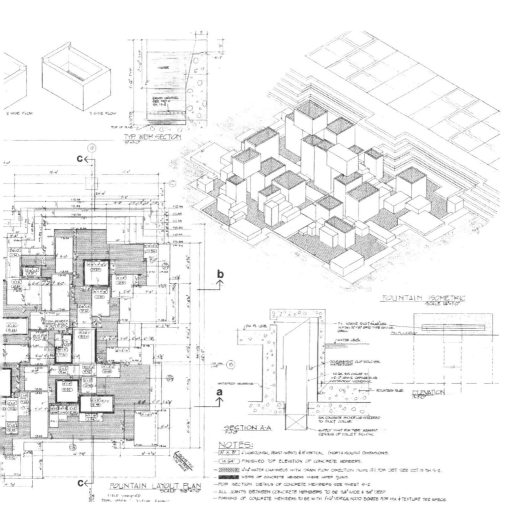

FOUNTAIN LAYOUT PLAN
SCALE 3/8"=1'-0"

TYP WEIR SECTION

FOUNTAIN ISOMETRIC
SCALE 1/4"=1'-0"

SECTION A-A

ELEVATION
TYP

NOTES:

FIG. 73:
Even devoid of water, the fountain
enticed children during the
Denver Public Schools' annual
Shakespeare Festival, in May 2003.

The Third Fountain

Construction of the final block did not take place until after the first
block was completed (in 1973) and the second was nearing completion. Reflecting on this phase of the design, Shirai, who, together
with Nishita, had worked extensively on the first two blocks, noted
that Halprin assigned another junior staff member to assist him with
the fountain studies and design development. The result, Shirai suggested, was "a compromise" to the design's consistency and expression.[6] Unlike the two earlier fountains, which were conceived as
features in plaza spaces, the third and final fountain was integrated
into the park's perimeter edge, creating an entry feature at the corner
of Arapahoe and Eighteenth streets, where its sounds enticed people
to enter Skyline Park. [FIG. 74] Appearing to be part of the retaining
wall that created the spatial boundary to the entry plaza, this fountain
was made up of stratified layers, extruded in slabs and cascading
from the berm and wall along Arapahoe Street. Despite the addition
of a new design team member, studies for this fountain reflect a style
reminiscent of the fountain on the middle block. The basic vocabulary
of the block forms continued through the design development process, but took on increasing complexity as other designers worked
on the project.

View of East Fountain on Block 16
Skyline Park   Denver, Colorado
Sept. 17 1970

Lawrence Halprin & Associates

FIG. 74:
This view shows the eastern
entrance from Eighteenth
Street into Skyline Park, with
the fountain at the right tightly
integrated into the wall bordering
the park along Arapahoe Street.

FIG. 75:
Nishita rendered this drawing,
in sepia marker on white
trace, in September 1970 for
a design presentation. It shows
the block between Eighteenth
and Seventeenth streets
in a view looking westward.

FIG. 76:
This study expresses a transition
from the presentation drawing
and forms a bridge to the final
design idea of layers and pools.

Its tiers and layers, seen in figure 77, distinguish this last
fountain from the two earlier ones. These layers adopted the six-
inch module of the cast-in-place concrete work applied to the park's
walls, stairs, and seating (as described in chapter 4). Interestingly,
the design development studies concentrated primarily on the
articulation of the fountain's overall form rather than its relationship
to human scale.

An early presentation drawing by Nishita from September
1970 shows the fountain in the position it maintained throughout;
its form is rendered as a rectilinear basin with stepped layers
descending into the pool. The evolution of this first idea offers insight
into the office's design process. [FIG. 75]

The study sketch plan in figure 76 shows a series of pools
and concrete platforms arranged in a staggered or alternating rhythm,

FIG. 77:
A view of the fountain near
the entrance at Eighteenth
Street reveals its tiers and
interactive nature.

which ultimately influenced the finished form—a fountain that masterfully melds into the contiguous berm and the system of concrete
retaining and stepped walls. Playful and engaging, the fountain drew
people into the park and invited them to explore by stepping and
climbing within the water's flow. [FIGS. 76, 77]

When given built form, Halprin's design philosophy
expressed his largesse. As illustrated by the distinct character of the
park's three fountain designs, the urban environments Halprin's firm
created, especially those associated with water, were open to multiple interpretations and uses, inviting people to engage with the place
and each other. As he concluded in *Cities*:

> The sense of water in the city and our great empathy with it is in
> no small measure related to the qualities of motion, both visual
> and audible. Fountains are exciting to us because they move
> and gyrate; cascades fall and the spray of droplets, caught
> like streaks of light in the sun, are the very essence of motion
> traced through their trajectory. The motion of fountains and
> the qualities of water effects can be programmed [to achieve]
> the sense of sound and the qualities which water generates.[7]

6

Skyline
Park's Life

The static conception of society and its image of the
city has given way to a conception of fluidity, of constant
change. Our great mission is, I believe, to deal with
change, to recognize it as an essential element in our time
and accept its implications. Since our ideal for the city
is uncertain, what we need to strive for is an environment
designed for the process of creative living.
—Lawrence Halprin, *Cities*

The implications of change Halprin referred to in *Cities* were not
so kind to Skyline Park, which underwent a sweeping demolition
commencing in May 2003. The decision by the city and county of
Denver to redesign and "preserve" parts of Skyline Park happened
gradually, in step with the processes of decline and the shift in public perception of the park's role and value. Initially, Denver's citizens
and businesses welcomed and celebrated the park, and it was
heavily used. The early days were heady; DURA took great pride in
the success of the Skyline Urban Renewal Project. In a promotional
book about this effort, it described Skyline Park as "a restful spot
in the center of a major metropolis" that offered "hurried shoppers,
city dwellers, tourists and office workers on lunch or coffee break
a place where, for a moment, they can escape from the everyday
world and enjoy the glories of Colorado's ever-changing seasons."
The publication elaborated:

During the summer and fall, it's not uncommon to find a small
band playing an impromptu jazz concert before hundreds of
appreciative onlookers enjoying the warm sun and music.
Office employees lounge in the park. Children wade in the
fountains. Executives stroll through the park, leaving the
cares of the office behind for an instant. Even in the winter
and early spring, the warm sunshine encourages city dwellers
to walk in the park.[1]

As business leaders and city officials had hoped, Skyline Park
became the centerpiece of downtown's redevelopment. It offered
quiet spots to rest, places for staged events and programs, and set-
tings for impromptu gatherings and lunchtime concerts.[2] The park
matured; trees grew, and the fountains flowed and pleased visitors.
[FIG. 78] In fact, in some ways its very success bred its demise; Skyline
Park catalyzed development, and these new additions to the urban
fabric and milieu eventually overshadowed or subsumed this small
but significant public space. As downtown was rejuvenated, the real
estate surrounding the park increased in value. Citizens, business
groups, and property owners desired more from the adjacent park,
prompting a call for change that led to several studies and reports,
and ultimately to the renovation.

     Several threads weave the story of the park's decline and
suggest "points of vulnerability" that eventually led to its demise. It may
seem strange to speak of a landscape solidly constructed from impec-
cably cast monolithic concrete as vulnerable, yet like most designed
landscapes, without adequate care it was also ephemeral. Skyline
Park's vulnerability to pressures from market and development forces
manifested at several levels, related to its geographic location in the
center of the city; to planning and design decisions for subsequent
developments nearby or adjacent to the park; to the rising value of
commercial land adjacent to the park and throughout the redevelopment area; to inadequate maintenance; to a decline in programming

FIG. 78:
In 1990 Skyline Park's harmonious ambience emanated from mature trees, shaded lawns, sparkling fountains, and plenty of visitors who enjoyed both sponsored and spontaneous activities in the park's spaces, such as those seen here.

and efforts to activate the park; and finally, to negative public perceptions about its safety, design style, and significance.[3]

One of the earliest challenges to the park's substance occurred when phased development of property adjacent to the park failed to adhere to the original master plan. Unlike the sympathetic relationship between the park and the Park Central Building, where the designers collaborated to bring the vision of the master plan into form, development along the northern edge of the subsequent two blocks was less successful in upholding the park's cornerstone ideals for mixed use, access, and harmonious design relationships. Particularly unfortunate was the development along the middle block between Seventeenth and Eighteenth streets where the park is flanked for nearly half the length by a parking garage. This defied the idea of shops or commercial storefronts lining the park to activate it and draw people along and into it.

Moreover, the moderately successful execution of an elevated circulation system at the Park Central Building failed to be repeated. The master plan's vision of an elevated pedestrian system quickly became obsolete, even though some higher-level elements connected to Skyline Park. In the third block, for instance, the park led to a second-level plaza area above the parking garage. The deck—private property—was typically chained off to pedestrian access at the bottom of these stairs, however. Visitors seldom defied this to move up to the plaza and the areas to which it connected. Despite attempts to introduce the elevated pedestrian system in the development around Skyline Park, this "revolutionary" urban planning idea quickly became outdated, leaving a disjointed set of elevated plazas and walkways that became underused, residual spaces. It is possible that the attempts to connect into this system via Skyline Park inadvertently undermined the park's form and relevance.

Another urban planning gesture that ultimately diminished the park's impact and prominence was the development of the Sixteenth Street Mall. Oriented perpendicular to Skyline Park, this dynamic commercial corridor and movement system intersected the park near the D & F Tower. The Denver transit mall design and planning team had projected to "transform Sixteenth Street between Broadway and Larimer" through a "unifying theme and common identity for the street while protecting its distinctive personality" of diverse and memorable spaces and functions.[4] Eventually, however, the success of and interest in the mall negatively affected the park. Skyline Park's quiet spaces for relaxation and respite along this urban spine began to fall from favor, becoming less viable as the antidote to the bustle of the transit mall. Its role as an urban space was not fully understood or supported; event programming by the city and county of Denver and the Downtown Denver Partnership (DDP) waned, as did routine maintenance.

In such a highly structured park as Skyline, the effects of diminishing maintenance posed problems in several areas. The two issues that became most troubling were the fountains and the plantings. The concrete and paved hardscape of the park required minimal maintenance; it was sturdy and well constructed. Generally, maintenance needs were met for standard snow, litter, and graffiti removal. Nonetheless, vandalism did damage some concrete elements and built-in amenities, such as the drinking fountains. [FIG. 79]

Halprin noted in *Cities*, "A city, like a forest, is a delicately balanced ecosystem, always in transition."[5] This process of dynamic change—even on a superficial level—challenged those in charge of maintenance. At Skyline Park, the fountains and plantings suffered due to reduced care and decreased funds allocated to maintenance. At the time of installation, trees were planted fairly close together with an understory of shrubs and groundcover, and swathes of turf on the berms. During periods when the irrigation system failed, plants went without water; this exacted harsh tolls, given the fact that Denver has little summer rain to compensate. Dryness and overuse affected the grassy areas. As trees reached maturity, welcome areas of dense shade appealed to visitors, but stunted the growth of understory plants below that needed more sun. Trees and shrubs were not trimmed or thinned, giving a sense of benign neglect as plants evolved through natural attrition or simply grew out of hand. [FIG. 80]

FIG. 79:
A decline in trash removal and maintenance, as well as vandalism affected the park; this drinking fountain is one of the worst examples of physical damage to elements within the park.

FIG. 80:
This photo from May 2003 of a sign ironically imploring visitors to "keep off the grass" shows the bare dirt resulting from a distinct lack of upkeep that contributed to the decline in public perception of the park.

The engineered water systems for the three fountains required timely maintenance and updating, which didn't always occur, whether from lack of funds or lack of awareness of certain needs. It is difficult to determine the full extent of the problems attached to the fountains, but one anecdote may help convey the factors that influenced the city's decision to alter the park's design. The first fountain between Fifteenth and Sixteenth streets worked well when it was first installed, but by the early 2000s its mechanisms were in need of an overhaul. Their age affected the fountain operations and, more subtly, impacted an adjacent commercial enterprise. The Palomino Restaurant, now closed, was located on the ground floor of the Park Central Building near the Sixteenth Street Mall. Sometime in the mid 1990s it opened an outdoor dining terrace that abutted the edge of the park, in close proximity to the plaza area and the first fountain. When the fountain operated (which was by this time no longer on a daily basis), the aged pump system caused wine glasses to vibrate on the tables of both inside and outside dining areas. The Palomino management argued that this diminished patronage and thus profits, and filed complaints with the city. The fountain could probably have been fixed by an upgrade of the mechanisms. That this route was not taken suggests that the Palomino management's argument of economic hardship carried political ramifications. It also points to the powerful constituency of local business owners, who in general advocated for changes in the park, including removing this offending fountain, as a way of updating its image and renewing interest in local businesses.[6]

Skyline Park became vulnerable politically. The DDP, a powerful consortium of business leaders, property owners, and commercial enterprise advocates, partnered with the city to begin exploring changes in Skyline Park that supported their goals for economic improvements. Like DURA, which conceived of the downtown redevelopment and sought catalysts for positive change in the 1960s and 1970s, the DDP sought to bring greater financial benefits to the area and to support revenue-generating initiatives. For the DDP and its constituents, the time had come to "revamp" Skyline Park. Aside from acting out of commercial interests, the partnership was also responding to the worn-out appearance of the park, concerns about some of the people who frequented it, and the sense

FIG. 81:
Perceptions of the park's safety were influenced by the presence of less socially acceptable people, such as skateboarders or groups of young punks, seen here seated on the plaza wall near the Palomino Restaurant and the Sixteenth Street Mall.

FIG. 82:
Skateboarders of all ages found the park's walls and ramps irresistible.

that it would benefit from a private/public partnership like the one that spearheaded the successful redesign of Bryant Park in New York City (completed in 1992).

For the DDP and the public, the social shift in park users was an impetus for change. Amongst planners and designers, it is fairly well known that an urban space vacated by one group will be adopted by another, especially with a decline in "eyes on the street," which provide a sense of owner- ship and support the maintenance and cultural worth of a place.[7] In the case of Skyline Park, as "acceptable" users flowed toward the mall, the park became a destination for young "mall rats," a haven for the homeless, and a hidden zone for socially outré behavior such as drug use. One teenager interviewed by the author spoke frankly about Skyline Park, calling it "a good place to chill....It's not busy like the mall, and no one hassles you here...no gangs, no fights, no bad stuff"; this park is "part of Denver's history and no one should...tear out history!"[8] Skateboarders commanded the ramps and walls of the park, and other "undesirable" users—youth with colored hair, chains, and punk clothing, and homeless or indigent people—became a vis- ible social presence. The park came to be thought of as dangerous, prompting visitors to become hyperaware; ultimately, the park's character allegedly scared off locals and visitors who would pay for goods and services. [FIGS. 81, 82]

As William Whyte asserted in his important book *The Social Life of Small Urban Spaces*, "The best way to handle the problem

of undesirables is to make a place attractive to everyone else." He also suggested that "undesirable" was perhaps a misnomer and that a preoccupation with ridding a site of a group of people is really a symptom of another problem.[9] It is revealing that even after the new design was installed, homeless people still sleep on the park's benches. But no one would foretell that in the excitement of sponsoring a new vision for the park; there was a clear political will by the mid-1990s for Skyline Park to be redesigned. [FIG. 83]

FIG. 83:
Despite the stated goals and appearance of the redesign, the park still offers places for homeless citizens to sit, rest, or sleep.

Apart from the park's physical and social decline, there was also the sense among local business constituents and city officials that the Halprin design had become dated, evincing a style that no longer met the image of downtown Denver. This argument is interesting, as it brings up issues of taste and of understanding the "style" of Halprin's design. Skyline Park's abstract, hard-edged, concrete forms and sculptural expressions did not mesh with popular conceptions of parks as grassy, leafy, rolling terrain, reminiscent of natural meadows. Nor did it meet normative criteria for plazas, as it was planted with trees, shrubs, and other plants. In the end, some of the design's attributes also became liabilities.

The berms along Arapahoe Street, which once created a sense of oasis by masking unpleasant downtown streets, now served to keep the park isolated and hidden from a rejuvenated and active urban environment to which it needed connection. There was no perimeter sidewalk along the Arapahoe Street edge, and park visitors were effectively cut off from the street within the park's linear spaces; the lowered ground plane of the park, although only a short distance down, contributed to this sense of isolation, because visitors couldn't register the adjacent street.[10] The *Rocky Mountain News* stated in an editorial on September 5, 2002:

> Unfortunately designer Lawrence Halprin used a plan that might have seemed like a good idea at the time but has since failed… the creation of spaces designed to offer the pedestrian some refuge from nearby vehicular traffic by putting them at different levels. Such isolation might seem attractive in the abstract but in practice it doesn't work. Skyline Park, for instance, is a hard surfaced, sunken canyon separated by berms from the traffic and providing nooks and crannies that appeal more to drug dealers, thugs, and layabouts than to ordinary citizens.… The situation is aggravated by poor lighting and chokepoints that seem to limit access. Ordinary citizens, women in particular, instinctively shy from it because of the short sightlines and the justified sense of menace the isolation engenders.[11]

In this climate, the thirty-year-old park once again became the focal point of efforts to enliven and rejuvenate this core area of Denver's urban fabric. In the late 1990s and early 2000s, the city sought advice by commissioning new master plan and feasibility studies, notably those by Design Workshop of Denver (1997) and Urban Strategies/Greenberg Consultants of Toronto, Canada (2001).[12] In 1998 Denver voters approved a bond issue of one hundred million dollars in general allocation funds that included Skyline Park. The city administration under Mayor Wellington Webb "committed $3 million to demolish Skyline Park and replace it with…another park!" with an additional eight to twelve million for the redesign to be done in stages.[13] In 2001 the city and county of Denver announced a national Request for Qualifications to redesign the park. Over forty

firms submitted proposals.[14] The review committee asked numerous
questions of those selected for interviews, including some directed at
the issue of preservation, such as the following: "Several historians
and preservationists see Skyline Park as a valuable representation
of Lawrence Halprin's work. If you were to receive the commission
for the redesign of Skyline Park, how would you approach this view-
point? Do you believe that any of that legacy can be (or should be)
accurately accommodated in the new plan? If so, how? If not, why?"[15]

Clearly, by this point the decision had been made to move
ahead with renovations, yet there were still public hearings and
a mounting pressure from interest groups to preserve Halprin's design.
Too late and woefully unprepared, the Friends of Skyline Park tried to
shift the tide.[16] In addition to local efforts, the Washington, D.C.–based
Cultural Landscape Foundation got involved by publishing essays on
its website and in national and regional trade publications. Locally,
a movement to document the park's current conditions and assess its
integrity and design significance became attractive as a modest goal.

As a result of mounting pressure from local and national
groups, Halprin himself became involved when he convened a Skyline
Park Take Part workshop, held on May 31, 2002, at his office in San
Francisco. Supporting Halprin were Dee Mullen and Paul Scardina
from his office, while the Denver participants included James Mejia of
Denver's Department of Parks and Recreation; Ann Mullins, a Denver
landscape architect with a specialty in preservation; architect and
urban designer David Tryba of David Owen Tryba Associates, the local
lead architect for Thomas Balsley Associates, New York City; and
Balsley himself, the landscape architect and urban designer selected
to redesign the park. The goal for the workshop was "to use the day
to reexamine the Park, develop a new sensitivity about it, and reach
consensus among ourselves."[17] The exercise led to a certain uneasy
consensus, with the results documented in the *Report: One Day Skyline
Park Workshop* and a notated plan. The thinking reflected a strategic
solution for minor modifications to the existing park to accommodate

necessary changes. Much of the original design was maintained, with adaptations to meet new criteria, such as opening up paths through the berm along Arapahoe Street. It effectively updated the design and addressed concerns in a thoughtful and feasible manner. Marking a low point in the public process, this proposal was set aside, and little of it made its way into the new design. The most obvious design solution that was adopted by Thomas Balsley Associates is the treatment of the edge along Arapahoe Street, where one lane of traffic was removed to accommodate a new sidewalk and on-street parking, with more openings and direct access at grade into the park. [FIG. 85]

Despite insufficient budget allocations that prevented construction of the full vision the redesign has generated considerable interest and support. Skyline Park's new state appears to have met goals identified by the city and its constituents, including local businesses and the DDP. A higher level of commitment to the park by key players such as the DDP and adjacent private businesses has

led to a renewed programming of the space, which hosts concerts and other events, and more diligent maintenance and management. The new park is considerably less sculptural than its predecessor; the site is almost uniformly raised to an even grade, with flat lawns that contain some visual elements introducing height and variation. One immediately obvious drawback to this is that the below-grade parking entrance and egress so carefully screened from view in Halprin's work are now quite visible from within the park. [FIG. 84]

Two fountains—those in the blocks east of the Sixteenth Street Mall—were kept and are operative, though they are not running at full capacity of water volume. From a design standpoint, their context is radically

FIG. 84:
A new structure housing restrooms and an information center sits near the Sixteenth Street Mall. With the ground plane raised to match adjacent grades and the berms removed, it is easy to see cars exiting the parking garage.

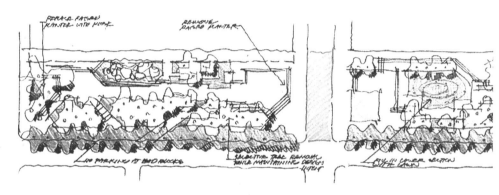

The workshop document
introduced the plan, noting,
"The following modifications,
if sensitively implemented,
will not compromise the essential
and core design principals
[sic.] of the original design
concepts of the Halprin design
for Skyline Park."

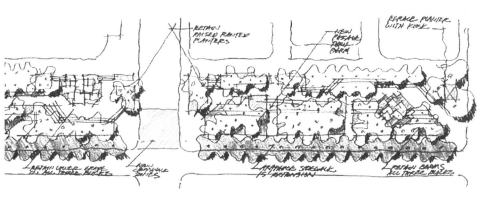

compromise the essential and core design principals of the original design concepts

...ntained except as noted below.
electrical systems as appropriate

of the park.
...pathway connections between the new sidewalks and the interior areas of the park.
...g 17 St. Remove raised planter on west side of 16th St.

...be removed for health reasons they should be replaced in kind to maintain design intent.
...area and NOT dispersed throughout park.

...n streets
...he original design approach.

These notes and the plan/diagram above
are an outgrowth of our workshop of 5/21/or
in San Francisco.

Lawrence Halprin

altered, and their material a stark contrast to the expensive sandstone paving and granite and white marble used for seat walls and other elements in the new design (see page 119, figure 88).

Some trees were also kept, notably many honeylocusts along Arapahoe Street and a few selected trees at the ends of each block, providing a sense of maturity to otherwise immature planting and new beds of perennials and grasses.

There are a few food stands within the park, and an information kiosk and restrooms are located in a new, modern structure just off the Sixteenth Street Mall near the area where the first fountain once stood. Unlike the earlier design, the present solution feels like it could be anywhere—in any city in the country.

Sites generate and hold value for a culture or group of people when they offer enduring meaning or function as a touchstone to an era or event. Halprin wrote in *Cities*:

> We need, in cities, buildings [and landscapes] of different ages, reflecting the taste and culture of different periods, reminding us of our past as well as our future. Some buildings are beautiful or striking enough to have their most useful periods artificially extended by preservation—almost like seeds of trees in a forest—so that succeeding generations can enjoy them, and through them maintain a sense of continuity with the past.[18]

When talking about the preservation of designed landscapes, Halprin asked: "Is the site in some way essential to the identity and life of the city it's in? Is it exemplary design? Does it in some way represent the best of a designer's works, or offer value to the city in some unparalleled way?" He believed that "at its best landscape architecture is an art form" and suggested assessing whether the site had merit as an artistic expression. Finally, he noted that examples of different periods ought to be preserved. This required educating the public about such places and offering frameworks for critical evaluation.[19]

With these guidelines in mind, how does one reflect on Halprin's design of Skyline Park? The park represented a masterful rendition of his ideas and stood as a singular landscape example of its era in Denver. William Thompson of *Landscape Architecture* stated, "Built works by modern masters have been dropping like ninepins all over the country. Some, like Skyline Park in Denver, have been more or less obliterated and replaced by more acceptable, if terminally bland, designs."[20] Mary Chandler, a local architecture critic quite familiar with the Skyline Park saga, wondered, "Will its bland replacement please anyone but adjacent business owners?"[21]

The demolition of the park has resulted in an untold loss—an erasure of urban memory. Fortunately, images and records of the park are preserved for posterity through documentation efforts, discussed in the next chapter. The final challenge, begun here, is to tell the site's stories and instill civic value through understanding the significance of its modernist landscape design for that place and that time, and for the people who never visited Skyline Park.

7

Documentation of the Site for the Historic American Landscapes Survey

In retrospect, I was designing prequels. I was setting
the stage for a return to downtowns. Now…we find
that people have returned to cities and the cities have
grown up and out and sometimes lost track of
the open space networks that knit them together.
—Lawrence Halprin

Entering Skyline Park one hot morning in early May 2003, a small crew
of students from the University of Colorado Denver began their daunt-
ing two-and-a-half-week mission to document the park's "as-built"
conditions to prepare a submission for HALS through the National Park
Service Intermountain Region office.[1] The team's work, supported by
an emergency documentation grant from the Colorado State Historical
Fund, represented the first landscape in the state of Colorado—and the
first modernist landscape in America—accepted for HALS.[2]

 The team found that the park overall was structurally sound,
with relatively little visible damage to major features, elements,
or surfaces. Given the urban circumstances and the extent of the
built form, Skyline Park seemed largely intact, with a high level of
design integrity. [FIG. 86] The findings suggested that the declared
need to alter or demolish the park was based on political rather than
functional concerns.

Damage and wear to the park were evident, however, and diminished maintenance and care had obviously taken their toll. In some areas the paving was cracked and brick surfaces had become uneven where the pavers had lifted off their concrete base. Edges of some of the lower concrete walls and stairs were abraded and discolored by hard use from skateboards sliding along them.

One of the drinking fountains built into the cast-in-place wall looked like it had been beaten with a sledgehammer (see page 105, figure 79). Several lights no longer functioned, and the built-in trash cans had long since been sealed in favor of off-the-shelf freestanding receptacles. The city had also added railings and signage, many of which now sported graffiti. More serious damage was discovered in the pump mechanisms of the fountains, which were malfunctioning, especially in the block between Fifteenth and Sixteenth streets. The greatest decline from the park's heyday, however, was evident in the plantings, with overgrown, crowded, and dead trees; little or no understory; and formerly lush planted areas reduced to straggly shrubs, dying turf, and dirt. [FIG. 87]

As noted in the previous chapter, supporters of Skyline Park had fought a losing battle against a public perception of the park being old and in ill repair, out of style, dangerous, and inhabited by unsavory characters. Various studies, an infusion of funding from the city, and a redesign signaled the end for the park as designed by Halprin. Preservationists prepared for a wholesale scrapping of the park, though in the end the redesign kept a few walls and two of the fountains, all woefully out of context in the new park. [FIG. 88]

FIG. 86:
Aerial view of Skyline Park's central block, showing the fountain at its eastern end (May 2003).

FIG. 87:
Planting in the park suffered greatly from lack of attention and maintenance. Although the junipers tolerated the conditions, other planting suffered; this tree stump was never removed nor the tree replaced, indicative of long-term neglect.

In this charged atmosphere, when restoring or rehabilitating the park was no longer a viable option, a group of supporters, spearheaded by local landscape architect Ann Mullins, submitted an emergency grant request to document the park to the Colorado State Historical Fund. The receipt of these funds allowed for the documentation team to quickly coalesce and get to work. [FIGS. 89, 90] Without the grant, the park in essence would have disappeared without record, and its preserved parts would have had even less relevance than they do today.

The last-minute timing of the grant underscored the project's urgency and required a tight orchestration of tasks. Once organized, the team had just over two weeks to complete the measurements and field documentation before demolition was scheduled to begin. Efficiency and accuracy were critical to meeting the documentation goals. To expedite the process, the team obtained a set of full-size reproductions of the construction documents created by Lawrence Halprin & Associates, which they used to note current field conditions and changes to the original design. Each sheet in the original Construction Drawings set was hand drawn in ink, pencil, or plastic lead on mylar.[3] Halprin's designers and draftsmen initialed the title blocks, thus providing a record of those involved in the project. The firm's originals—and thus most of the contractor's field

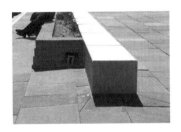

FIG. 88:
A residual bit of a Halprin-era wall, a token preservation gesture, is patently incongruous with the white marble and herbaceous plantings in the redesigned park, seen here along the Sixteenth Street Mall edge of the first block (2007).

sets—were updated to show adjustments and revisions that occurred on site during construction. A final "as-built" record set of the construction drawings was submitted to the city of Denver.

The documentation team used blueprint copies of these as-built drawings to note changes and measure for differences and variations from the as-built conditions.[4] This not only allowed the team to ascertain the overall extant quality of the park's design and features, it enabled them to correlate Halprin's design intentions to the as-built circumstances, and then to determine the completeness or integrity of the extant conditions against this basis.[5]

The documentation package submitted to HALS built on the work conducted during those busy two weeks, though it took many months of work by many individuals.[6] Students taking part in the project learned to read a site; to discover clues identifying the patterns of use and abuse; to see nuances of the built work, such as the various textures of the concrete; to appreciate the quality of thoughtfully conceived details; to understand the difference between the original planting intent and the ravages of time; and perhaps most importantly, to see the site as an intentional design replete with subtlety and tactile experience.

The completed HALS package was modeled on the federal Historic American Buildings Survey (HABS) and Historic American Engineering Record (HAER) work, but with some specific adjustments for landscape, such as rendering practices and Field Notes components. Final deliverables included a detailed history of the park with a biography of Halprin, accompanied by an extensive bibliography on Halprin, as well as on Skyline Park. Deliverables also included ink on mylar measured drawings typical for similar HABS and HAER projects.[7] [FIGS. 91, 94]

The HALS submission also included black-and-white archival photographs by Gifford Ewing, with a map noting the positions in the park from which they were shot, a complete photo log, and a set of archived and numbered large-format negatives.[8] Supporting these standard submission components was an extensive Field Notes packet, which included copies of the Halprin construction drawings, a set of which were annotated in the field; numerous logged and labeled slides and color photographs; field sketches of the park during the documentation; and a collection of historical documents, such as the various master plan proposals, newspaper clippings, and other brochures and flyers that support the story of Skyline Park.[9] The HALS

Field Notes also included a video titled *Skyline Park: Urbane Intention and Hard-Edged Grace*, which captured aspects of movement so relevant to Halprin, showing what it once was like to move through the park, with eddies and flows of people, and images of the park's qualities.[10] It also contains documentary footage of interviews with key players in the Skyline Park saga, such as city council representative Elbra Wedgworth. The video and commentary it contains are a poignant and lasting record of the time and the ideas and circumstances

FIG. 89:
The kick-off meeting for the documentation grant work took place at Mullins's home in April 2003. The team included landscape architect Ann Mullins, investigative team leader Ann Komara, local photographer Gifford Ewing, and videographer Eric Awltman.

FIG. 90:
The documentation process included many University of Colorado students. Two Ph.D. students, Pearl Wang and Manish Chalana, lead teams and spearheaded much of the field work; here they are measuring and sketching the fountain in front of the Park Central Building.

that made the park successful, as well as the various opinions about its final state and the reasons that led to its demise.

The final submission, titled HALS-CO-01, serves as a complement to this publication, along with the Halprin Collection in the Architectural Archives at the University of Pennsylvania. Skyline Park, a sculptural, engaging urban oasis envisioned by Denver's leaders and created by designers imbued with Halprin's overarching vision, survived for thirty years, failing to stand the test of time. Thanks to the HALS documentation, it can still be admired and studied, though

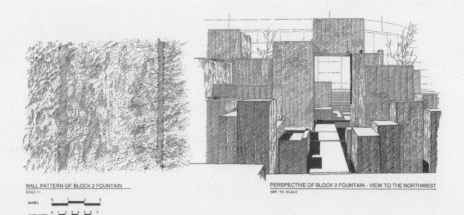

WALL PATTERN OF BLOCK 2 FOUNTAIN
SCALE 1:1

INCHES

CENTIMETERS

PERSPECTIVE OF BLOCK 2 FOUNTAIN - VIEW TO THE NORTHWEST
NOT TO SCALE

FIG. 91, top:
HALS drawings for the fountain
in the central block reveal its
sculptural composition and
suggest the texture of the concrete
surface resulting from the boards
used to form it in place. A special
drawing for this fountain translated
a rubbing of the concrete surface
to show the texture of the exposed
aggregate finish and dimension
of the boards.

FIG. 92, middle:
An exhibition titled *Skyline Park
1973–2003* at the University
of Colorado Denver's College
of Architecture and Planning
celebrated the completion of the
HALS documentation in February
2006. Open to the public, this
retrospective of the documentation
products and process generated
commentary and reflections
about the park.

FIG. 93, bottom:
Viewed from the Eighteenth Street
entrance, Skyline Park beckons
visitors to enter for a lingering
walk through its spaces a few days
before its demolition.

without the magic of the dappled shade, the glistening fountains, or the daily interaction and movement of visitors that Halprin deemed essential to enhancing the urban condition. [FIG. 92]

Mary Chandler wrote in the *Rocky Mountain News*, "In a sense, those working to document the park won their own sort of battle, with cameras, pens and paper. The field notes and drawings are a clear reminder of the technical intelligence of Halprin's design. But the photographs, by Denver-based Gifford Ewing, are so evocative they place a viewer back in the park."[11] Stephen Bruce Gale, a local architect, stated, "The students have…gained vicarious insight into one of the modern movement's masters and preserved an aspect of his project's totality and effect for posterity to appreciate, and possibly re-consider in eras yet to come."[12] The reconfigured park today contains only remnants of Halprin's work in Denver; those who never saw Skyline Park in its heyday may appreciate a last glimpse of the dappled shade in this sculptural landscape, an urban oasis in the heart of Denver. [FIG. 93]

In reflection about his work at Skyline Park, Halprin wrote, in May of 2002:

> I always felt that it was important to capture the regional character of areas where I was planning and designing. I wanted to bring an "experiential equivalent" of the local quality and local materials into the city. I wanted to acknowledge important views and historic buildings and take advantage of memory and our innate sense of "rightness." These open spaces provide the lungs, circulation, and heart of the cities. They should receive ongoing treatments. If they've been ignored they may need healing treatments. But "city doctors" should also consider the Hippocratic oath. First, do no harm.[13]

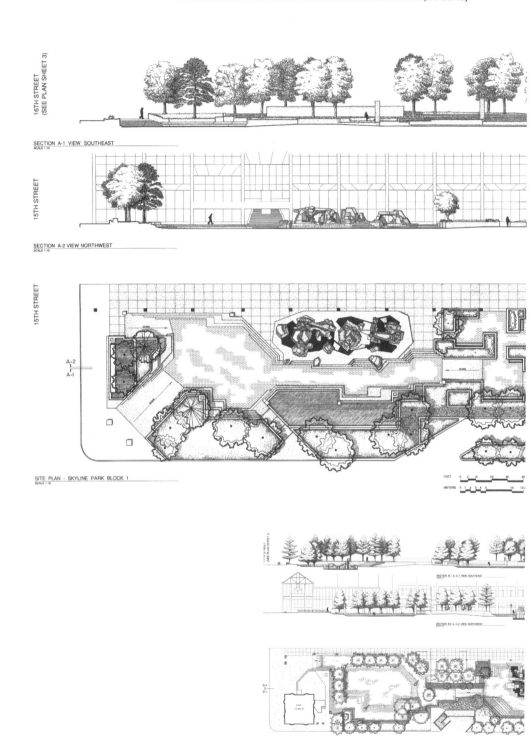

16TH STREET
(SEE PLAN SHEET 3)

SECTION A-1 VIEW SOUTHEAST
SCALE 1:10

15TH STREET

SECTION A-2 VIEW NORTHWEST
SCALE 1:10

15TH STREET

A-2
A-1

SITE PLAN - SKYLINE PARK BLOCK 1
SCALE 1:10

FEET   0   5   10   20   30   40
METERS 0 1 2 3 4 5   10   12.1

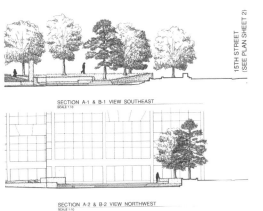

SECTION A-1 & B-1 VIEW SOUTHEAST
SCALE 1:10

SECTION A-2 & B-2 VIEW NORTHWEST
SCALE 1:10

FIG. 94:
The rendered site plan from the HALS documentation, which shows the whole of the park's three blocks complete with fountains, hardscape and walls, and planting.

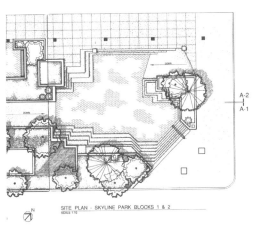

SITE PLAN - SKYLINE PARK BLOCKS 1 & 2
SCALE 1:10

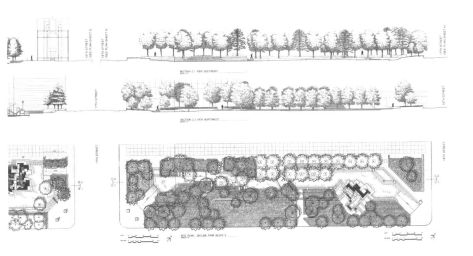

Reflections on Skyline Park

Laurie D. Olin

Halprin was a great American. Like George Gershwin, another son of Jewish immigrants from Brooklyn, he was interested in popular culture and how to make public art that would resonate with life as it is lived today—that measured up to the classics of the past while being thoroughly modern. Halprin was interested in place, time, movement, and form. In the course of his career he tried numerous things, and along the way produced one iconic landscape after another. Skyline Park in Denver was one of those experiments that was destroyed just before people understood what a unique masterpiece it was. The perceived social problems that it seemed to engender had little to do with its physical design and everything to do with nearly universal social and economic problems in American cities at the end of the twentieth century; ethnic and racial prejudice; several decades of terrible planning decisions; bad architecture; suburban flight; and the abandonment of historic urban centers. Had Skyline Park survived for another five or ten years, it would have had a renaissance, as a new generation continues to move back into the rapidly changing district of town within which it was built.

Ironically, Halprin's design for Skyline Park was an infrastructure project intended to help encourage development and to give value to an urban renewal project on the edge of downtown Denver. After having torn down many blocks of nineteenth-century buildings, the planners and business community turned to Halprin for help. The plan for a park that emerged was a sequence of linear spaces extending for three blocks astride a proposed transit corridor on Sixteenth Street that had been identified by a concurrent plan by Wallace McHarg Roberts & Todd for the Regional Transportation District.

As in his innovative and now iconic projects in Portland, Oregon, and Seattle, Washington, with their fountains (see pages 14–15), Halprin's design was grounded in abstract references to the mountain landscape of the West. At Skyline Park, however, the design also drew upon forms reminiscent of indigenous and pre-Columbian architecture, but without the elaborate ornamental patterns that had been employed by Frank Lloyd Wright in the California work that Halprin knew. Because the three parcels were narrow and two were to have ramps leading to underground parking for adjacent office buildings, he chose to eliminate traditional curbside walkways along the streets and instead to use the interior of each parkway strip as both walkway and plaza, consciously buffering a major portion of the park from the street with substantial berms in one configuration or another. The three parts of the park were conceived both as retreats from the surroundings and as gathering and strolling places. In the 1970s and early 1980s they were successful, popular, and well used, as one can see in photographs from the time.

The imagery of the large central fountain in the southernmost block was clearly a melding of landform and pueblo, of the Rocky Mountains, mesas, and mission churches. The fountain was dry seasonally like many of the canyons and *arroyos* in the Four Corners region to the south and the basin and range territory to the west of Denver. In his autobiography Halprin states that he was particularly inspired by the large red sandstone formations near Denver in the foothills of the Front Range. These rocks are well known to local inhabitants, partly because the Works Progress Administration constructed a superb outdoor amphitheater—the Red Rocks Amphitheatre, still in use for summer concerts and performances—in one of the most accessible and handsome portions of this landscape during the Great Depression.

The fountain in the middle block often had more water and was largely and compulsively composed employing the contour and ledge technique first used by Halprin's office in the fountains in Portland and Seattle. At the time the grassy terraces and concrete walls were not the cliché they may seem today after having been copied by his own firm and endlessly by others around the world afterward. It also was consciously modern in its use of geometries in plan and section, inspired by the sculpture, painting, and architecture of the de Stijl movement and the International Style or the Bauhaus, with sequences of square, rectangular, cubic shapes, piers, blocks, and basins in overlapping, juxtaposed, asymmetrical clusters and groupings from which gushed and splashed water.

The third block seemed as much a meditation on Mayan ball courts and natural canyons as it was a physical manifestation of the "stroll," a ramble with small episodes, an abstracted dry stream with eddies. The linear stepped forms of pre-Columbian architecture in Central America had enchanted Wright and other early Californian designers as well. As he was to do on numerous occasions throughout his career, Halprin was borrowing liberally and comparing himself and his work to that of others, as well as indulging in an atavistic mood that was shared by many at the time who were embarking on what came to be called site sculpture and land art, such as Robert Smithson or Mary Miss. As at Lovejoy Plaza and the Ira Keller Fountain in Portland, the Skyline Park scheme made superb use of concrete. Halprin was demonstrating that in the hands of an artist the most humble or banal materials could be lovely. The concrete at the park was a wonderful color and texture and beautifully detailed.

There was no grand space in Skyline Park. This project offered instead a demonstration of Halprin's interest in turning earlier analytical work, especially his concept of motation in its various iterations, into a prescriptive device, and using its logic and insights to create or program a linked set of diverse places/experiences that could be enjoyed in isolation or as a continuum. Anyone who has ever attempted to design a linear park will recognize the issues and problems Halprin articulated so clearly in this work.

When the hoped-for development for the area surrounding the park finally arrived, it was in the form of bulky condominiums, slick or heavy-handed office buildings, shopping arcades, restaurants, and bars catering to suburbanites. Most of the buildings and visitors turned their backs on the park, which deteriorated and eventually filled up with the homeless and skateboarders. After a lengthy controversy Skyline Park has been demolished and replaced with a mediocre, meaningless, placeless set of lawns and furniture. This act of public vandalism has in turn caused controversy and not only reenergized the local preservation community that fought the park's redevelopment, but garnered such support for it that recent efforts to alter and rework to some degree the Sixteenth Street Mall, which crosses Skyline Park, were soundly stopped. "Not another Skyline" was the phrase used in public meetings. While Halprin's Skyline Park is no more, it is remembered fondly as a special place, once socially vibrant and handsome, exactly as imagined by one of America's greatest landscape architects and public artists.

Epilogue

Lawrence Halprin

At the end of a play there is an epilogue, and this is mine for the drama that has played out around Skyline Park in Denver.

When Skyline Park was designed and built, it was part of a great process of urban renewal that was going on throughout the United States. It was meant to generate new life in the downtown area and encourage citizens to get involved in the life of the city. It was also designed to represent the special regional character of Denver, with its great environmental resources and geological forms and colors.

In 2002 The Denver Parks and Recreation Department contacted me because of the great amount of interest, concern, and disagreement that was generated by controversies surrounding the future of the park. I certainly understand that after many years of use projects require some modifications to maintain them and bring them up to date. I was pleased that the city wanted my input, and I therefore offered to convene (pro bono) a one-day RSVP workshop in my San Francisco office with participants from Denver.

After a series of exercises that set program priorities, the individuals involved drew up their conceptual plans, and I summarized my feelings about which elements would be compatible with the original design. Tom Balsley drafted the summary concept plan, and I hand wrote my general notes at the bottom. My only concern was that the changes be done with care and sensitivity to the original design. I was saddened to hear that the public never saw this plan we had agreed on. From my perspective I felt it was a lost opportunity.

Now that the long fight to save the original Skyline Park is at an end and major destructive changes have been made,

I must say that I am disappointed that the attempt to preserve the park through modest modifications was lost. I am hopeful, however, that the time and effort that were spent are the beginning of a new era of appreciation for historic landscapes that mark our social and environmental evolution.

I am extremely pleased that recently some cities, such as Portland, Oregon, when faced with similar problems, have been able to carefully navigate the fine line between careful modification and protection of original design intent. In the future I believe that such thoughtful attention will become second nature when faced with such challenges. In that way, we can protect the special places that speak to our history and evolution.

I am extremely thankful that this monograph has captured the story of Skyline Park. I believe it offers lessons from the past and hope for the future.

Larry Halprin

FIG. 95:
Halprin painting at the Sea Ranch, 2008.

Acknowledgments

This book rests on the work of many people, beginning with Lawrence Halprin, who graced Denver with a park worth writing about. My colleague Ann Mullins spearheaded the documentation effort and in effect "saved" Skyline Park for future generations. Gene Bressler, former chair of the University of Colorado Denver Department of Landscape Architecture, encouraged and supported my work and that of our students, whose collective dedication to the documentation was instrumental. Several deserve direct recognition for work above and beyond the call: Manish Chalana and Pearl Wang dominated the documentation efforts; Mark Sullivan, Zach Peterson, and Sebastian Wielogorski did the beautiful Historic American Landscapes Survey (HALS) drawings. Cynthia Guajardo, my current research assistant par excellence, organized years of research materials—hundreds of photos and digital and archival files, thus making my writing easier and the production fluid. She listened and commiserated and cheered me on. This book would never have gotten finished without her.

Thanks also go to Kathleen McCormick, who edited a very rough manuscript, and Nicola Bednarek Brower, my editor at Princeton Architectural Press, who helped me refine and polish the work. Charles Birnbaum edited text and shared his knowledge and images; his belief in and vision for this book and the series reflect his dedication to preservation and the icons of modernism he champions. I am grateful for his partnership. Finally, I wish to thank the State Historical Fund (SHF), a program of History Colorado, for funding all phases of my work on this project, and Estella Cole, my project liaison at the SHF, who misses Halprin's Skyline Park.

Notes

Introduction

1. Marvin Hatami and Floyd Tanaka et al., *Urban Design and Development Study. Part 1: Urban Design Concept, and Part 2: Implementation Standards and Criteria* (Denver: March 1970).

2. Paul Foster and Barbara Gibson, *Denver's Skyline Park—A History* (Denver: City and County of Denver, 2000), 4.

3. Mark Johnson, "Skyline Park: Preservation Ethics and Public Space," in *Preserving Modern Landscape Architecture II—Making Postwar Landscape Visible*, eds. Charles Birnbaum, Jane Brown Gillette, and Nancy Slade (Washington, D.C.: Spacemaker Press, 2004), 42–49.

Chapter 1: Lawrence Halprin and Landscape Architecture

1. Douglas Martin, "Lawrence Halprin, Landscape Architect, Dies at 93," *New York Times*, October 28, 2009. http://www.nytimes.com/2009/10/28/arts/design/28halprin.html.

2. Martin, "Lawrence Halprin, Landscape Architect, Dies at 93." Anna Halprin noted, "The Roosevelt memorial was [his] favorite project…Partly because he had loving memories of Roosevelt, and partly because of the sheer difficulty of the task." See also: Lawrence Halprin, *The Franklin Delano Roosevelt Memorial* (San Francisco: Chronicle Books, 1997). Through the 1990s and 2000s Halprin remained involved in a few projects with the help of Dee Mullen and others from his office. Projects he completed in his later years include the Stern Grove Concert venue in San Francisco (2005), the Letterman Digital Arts Center (opened in 2005) in the Presidio in San Francisco's Golden Gate National Recreation Area, and the fifty-two-acre approach to the Falls in Yosemite National Park, which he began working on in 1996.

3. American Society of Landscape Architects, "ASLA Leaders Express: Leadership and Governance. Halprin Receives Michelangelo Award," ASLA, March 30, 2005 (accessed October 2005), http://www.asla.org/ContentDetail.aspx?id=5664&RMenuId=8&PageTitle=Leadership. See also: J. William Thompson, "From Landscape Architecture, Lawrence Halprin, FASLA, Is the First Winner of the Michelangelo Award, Given This Year by the Construction Specifications Institute." *ASLA Land Matters*, LAND Online, April 4, 2005, http://landarchives.asla.org/landsearch/archive/2005/0404/landmatters.html (accessed October 2011) and American Society of Landscape Architects, "ASLA Medals and Firm Awards," ASLA News, May 14, 2003 (accessed October 2005). http://www.asla.org/newslistingdetails.aspx?id=9124&terms=halprin. In 2003 the American Society of Landscape Architects selected Halprin "as the first recipient of the new ASLA Design Medal recognizing an individual landscape architect who has produced a body of exceptional design work at a sustained level for a period of at least ten years."

4. A list of Halprin projects subjected to threats of renovation or demolition can be found through The Cultural Landscape Foundation: http://www.tclf.org.

5. Jane Jacobs, *The Death and Life of Great American Cities* (New York: Random House Vintage Books, 1961).

6. Following is a selected list of key landscape architects practicing in the twentieth century: A. E. Bye, Garrett Eckbo, M. Paul Friedberg, Dan Kiley, James Rose, Robert Royston, Hideo Sasaki, John Simonds, and Robert Zion. The roster of landscape architects in practice contemporaneously with Halprin is extensive; a list can be obtained from the archives of the American Society of Landscape Architects (ASLA) in Washington, D.C. http://www.asla.org. Readers can also consult The Cultural Landscape Foundation website.

7. Halprin created several films in the 1970s and 1980s. In 1976 he and Anna created *How Sweet It Is* (RoundHouse, 1976), a film about dance and theater in the environment. That same year he made *Le Pink Grapefruit*, produced by Sue Yung Li Ikeda (RoundHouse, Phoenix Films, 1976), a film about the environment and art of Salvador Dali, which received a Special Jury Award at the 1976 San Francisco Film Festival.

8. William J. Thompson, "Master of Collaboration," *Landscape Architecture* 82/7 (July 1992): 64.

9. Lawrence Halprin, *A Life Spent Changing Places* (Philadelphia: University of Pennsylvania Press, 2011).

10. Highlights of Halprin's life and professional practice through 1986 are covered in an exhibition catalogue published by the

San Francisco Museum of Modern Art (SFMoMA) at the occasion of its 1986 exhibition *Lawrence Halprin: Changing Places* in a section titled "The Chronology." Lynn Creighton Neall, ed., *Lawrence Halprin: Changing Places* (San Francisco: SFMoMA, 1986), 114. Halprin's parents married in 1914. Halprin had one sister, Ruth (born in 1924). His father, Samuel, was "president of Landseas Scientific Instruments, and his mother, Rose (1896–1978), was president of Hadassah, the women's Zionist organization, and chairperson of the American branch of the Jewish Agency for Palestine." See the Jewish Women's Archive: Eric Goldstein, "Rose Luria Halprin," http://jwa.org/encyclopedia/article/halprin-rose-luria (accessed August 19, 2011).

11. Halprin, *A Life Spent Changing Places*, 8–18; 23–32. Halprin recalls his first trip abroad to Europe and Palestine in the late 1920s, and in a later section of this biography, speaks of his experiences in the kibbutz.

12. Lawrence Halprin & Associates, "Firm Profile Insert," *Engineering News-Record*, November 7, 1968. This profile includes Halprin's resume listing education, experience, honors, memberships, teaching, publications, and projects from his practice.

13. Benjamin Forgey, "Lawrence Halprin: Maker of Places and Living Spaces," *Smithsonian* 19/9 (Dec 1988): 162.

14. Neall, ed., *Lawrence Halprin: Changing Places*, 116. In the 1960s, Anna Halprin became "a major force in the dance world for her staging of avant-garde performances." See also: Anna S. Halprin, ed. Rachel Kaplan, *Moving Toward Life: Five Decades of Transformational Dance* (Hanover, NH: University Press of New England for Wesleyan University Press, 1995).

15. Lawrence Halprin, "The Choreography of Gardens," *Impulse* (1949). 32–34.

16. Lawrence Halprin, "Dialogue: Rawrence [sic] Halprin + Ching-Yu Chang," *Process Architecture No. 4*, ed. Ching-Yu Chang (Tokyo: Process Architecture Publishing, 1978), 247.

17. Thompson, "Master of Collaboration," 64.

18. Both Halprin and Wurster developed practices in California; they collaborated on a number of projects, including Halprin's home in Kentfield. Wurster became a leading figure in the movement known as the "Second Bay Tradition." Halprin, *A Life Spent Changing Places*, 46–48; 75.

19. Neall, ed., *Lawrence Halprin: Changing Places*, 115. Various sources offer conflicting dates for Halprin's period at Harvard's School of Design and for his military service. It is clear that he entered Harvard in 1942. Consensus is he enlisted in 1943, entered training, and saw service through 1945.

20. Halprin worked closely with Church, becoming an associate in the firm in 1947. In addition to their design collaborations, they co-authored articles such as "Backyard Gardens," *House Beautiful* (1947): np. See also: Thomas D. Church, *Gardens Are for People: How to Plan for Outdoor Living* (New York: Reinhold Publishing Corp., 1955) and Marc Treib, ed., *Modern Landscape Architecture: A Critical Review* (Cambridge: MIT Press, 1993).

21. See Halprin's selected project list from 1949 to 1986: "The Chronology," in Neill, ed., *Lawrence Halprin: Changing Places*, 116–149, and Halprin, A Life Spent Changing Places, 74–88; 97–112.

22. Benjamin Forgey, "Lawrence Halprin: Maker of Places and Living Spaces—the Landscapes That He Creates Are Based on a Combination of Science, Ecology, and All-Encompassing Humanity," *Smithsonian* 19, no. 9 (December 1988): 165.

23. Lawrence Halprin, *Cities* (Cambridge: The MIT Press, 1963, rev. ed. 1972), 9.

24. Forgey, "Lawrence Halprin," 166.

25. Neill, ed., *Lawrence Halprin: Changing Places*, 125.

26. Forgey, "Lawrence Halprin," 164–65.

27. *Process Architecture No. 4*, 241.

28. Forgey, "Lawrence Halprin," 166. Forgey called Nicollett Mall "another exercise in urban reclamation…one of the early major efforts to [successfully] return a traditional decaying city-center to pedestrians."

29. Lawrence Halprin, *Cities* (New York: Reinhold, 1963), 9.

30. Halprin, "My Design Process," in *Process Architecture No. 4*, 10–14.

31. For more on the Take Part process in Charlottesville, see Alison Bick Hirsch, *Lawrence Halprin: Choreographing Urban Experience*, dissertation for Ph.D. in historic preservation, University of Pennsylvania (2008). Halprin began the Charlottesville Mall project in 1973; construction was finished in late 1975.

32. Lawrence Halprin, *The RSVP Cycles* (New York: George Braziller, 1969) 1. *The RSVP Cycles* is dedicated to Halprin's wife, his partner in the development of this approach. For one of numerous reviews of the book see: Eugene Kupper, "Review Symposium: The RSVP Cycles…," *Urban Affairs Review* 6 (1971): 495.

33. Halprin, *The RSVP Cycles*, 1–2. Leslie, "Profile of Lawrence Halprin," 1996/2001 (site discontinued, accessed October, 2005). http://www.well.com/user/jacques/lawrencehalprin.html. During Leslie's interview, Halprin noted that of the five books he had then published on design, *The RSVP Cycles* was the one of which he was most proud.

34. Ibid., 2.

35. Halprin, "My Design Process," in *Process Architecture No. 4*, 14.

36. Halprin, *Cities*, 9.

Chapter 2: Conceiving the Park

1. C. H. Johnson, Jr., *The Daniels & Fisher Tower: A Presence of the Past* (Denver, Colorado: Tower Press, 1977), 22. Designed by architects Frederick J. Sterner and George Williamson,

the D & F Tower is a grand example of renaissance-revival architecture and an inexact replica of the celebrated Campanile of St. Mark's Basilica in Venice, Italy. It was Denver's tallest building until the 1953 construction of the twenty-three-story Mile High Center at Seventeenth Street and Broadway.

2. Foster and Gibson, *Denver's Skyline Park*, 2.

3. Donna McEnroe, *Denver Renewed—A History of the Denver Urban Renewal Authority* (Denver: The Denver Foundation and Alex B. Holland Memorial Fund, 1992), 37–39.

4. Foster and Gibson, *Denver's Skyline Park*, 3.

5. An early illustration of the expressway idea appeared in the *Denver Post: Empire*, June 24, 1956, n.p. Though similar transit ideas continued to appear in various plans, the expressway was finally rejected as financially unfeasible during the U.S. Department of Housing and Urban Development 1967 review of the Skyline Urban Renewal Plan. McEnroe, *Denver Renewed*, 225–27.

6. Foster and Gibson, *Denver's Skyline Park*, 3–5.

7. Ibid., 5–7.

8. McEnroe, *Denver Renewed*, 53.

9. Ibid., 110–13.

10. Real Estate Research Corporation, Abbott L. Nelson and Robert S. DeVoy, *Preliminary Economic and Marketability Analysis Phase 1 of Land Utilization and Marketability Study Skyline Urban Renewal Project, Project No. Colo. R-15, Denver, Colorado* (Chicago: RERC, Prepared for Denver Urban Renewal Authority, September 1965).

11. William H. Wilson, *The City Beautiful Movement* (Baltimore: Johns Hopkins University Press, 1989), 168–89.

12. The flood and its ramifications for urban redevelopment and DURA's decisions are well covered in McEnroe, *Denver Renewed*, 135–43.

13. Baume, Polivnick, Hatami, *Urban Design and Development Study Denver Skyline Renewal Area, Project COLO. No. R-15* (Denver, 1967), n.p.

14. McEnroe, *Denver Renewed*, 212; 253–64.

15. Ibid., 227. See also "Denver Skyline," *HUD Challenge* (April 1972): 27–30. This article states the project, a mixed-use improvement district plan, received a $33.2 million grant.

16. Hatami and Tanaka, *Urban Design and Development Study: Skyline Urban Renewal*.

17. Stuart Dawson recalled his work on the project: "The beautiful tower 'plugged' the corner of the massive D & F Building and was scheduled to be torn down along with the connecting adjacent buildings. Marve and I fought hard to keep the D & F Tower and with lots of client and finally public/developer support, it was saved. The plan called for a complementary three-block open space that seemed 'just right' and in scale with the handsome [tower]. We worried about the East-West orientation of the spaces because new buildings on the north side would necessarily cast serious shadows along the

entire three block plaza, and we did NOT feel that water features would be appropriate. Old Stan White axiom, fountains need sunlight." E-mail, Stuart O. Dawson, Sasaki Associates to Ann Komara, December 1, 2009.

18. Marvin Hatami and Associates, and Tanaka and Associates, *Feasibility Study for Skyline Park and Convention Center Parking Structures -Skyline Urban Renewal Project*, Colorado No. R-15 (Denver: Prepared for DURA by Marvin Hatami and Associates, and Tanaka and Associates, 1969).

19. Hatami and Tanaka, *Urban Design and Development Study*, Vol. 2, 50.

Chapter 3: The Master Plan—Connections and Infrastructure

1. Nilo Lindgren, "Riding a Revolution 1_1971," *Landscape Architecture* 64/3 (April 1974): 133–39; 190–91. See also Nilo Lindgren, "Riding a Revolution 2_1973," *Landscape Architecture* 64/3 (April 1974): 140–47.

2. Halprin, *A Life Spent Changing Places*, 146.

3. Ibid., 97; 111. Halprin notes the following employees in his office by the mid 1950s: Jean Walton, Sat Nishita, Pete Walker, Don Carter, Rich Haag, followed by Richard Vignolo, and then the graphic designer Tak Yamamoto. He noted also that many of his young employees arrived straight out of the University of California, Berkeley

4. Lindgren, "Riding a Revolution_1," 136. Nishita also worked on the Lovejoy and Ira Keller Fountains in Portland, Oregon.

5. Junji Shirai, e-mail message to Ann Komara, May 26, 2011. Shirai graduated in 1964 from the elite Waseda University, located in Shinjuku, Tokyo, with a master of architecture and a master of city planning. After a tour of the United States and a brief stint with Paolo Soleri at Arcosanti, he began working for Halprin's office in September 1968. He identified his signature "icon," which appears on many of the project drawings in the archives. At the time of our correspondence he was a senior consultant of the management team for Metropolitan Green Design and Technology in Singapore.

6. Junji Shirai, e-mail message to Ann Komara, 26 May, 2011. Shirai noted that he enjoyed a close working relationship with Sat Nishita; they continued their collaboration in Halprin's office on Heritage Park in Ft. Worth, Texas.

7. The Lawrence Halprin Collection, The Architectural Archives, The University of Pennsylvania, Philadelphia, Pennsylvania, (Halprin Archives). 014.I.A.4680. "LHA Skyline Park Critical Path" sheets, May through December, 1970. Notations on the office's Critical Path sheets for the Skyline Park project indicate billable hours totaled May through August 1970: Lawrence Halprin at 9.0; Sat Nishita at 22.5; Richard Vignola at 7.5; Junji Shirai at 132.0. This clearly delineates the team and its hierarchy.

8. Halprin Archives, flat drawing files, 014 II A 255.

9. Halprin Archives, 014.I.A.4920-.4921. An annotation on the notes in different pen and handwriting affirmed, "This is the way to go."

10. Halprin Archives, 014, box 159, folder: Skyline Urban Renewal. Letter from J. Robert Cameron, DURA, to Lawrence Halprin, March 11, 1970. Cameron paraphrases from *Urban Design and Development: Skyline Urban Renewal Project, Denver, Colorado. Project Colorado No. R-15*, vol. 1, 28.

11. Halprin Archives, box files, 014.I.A.4681. Design notes dated May 18, 1970, which state, "This is OK." and "After discussion with Sat/Junji on August 27" (written on a meeting note, referencing the study sketches).

12. Hatami and Tanaka, *Urban Design and Development Study*, Vol. 1, 28. The plan contained several images and a diagram illustrating this system across the whole Skyline Redevelopment Area.

13. Interview with George Hoover, project architect and former Muchow employee; currently professor of architecture at University of Colorado Denver, May 2008. The Architectural Archives for William C. Muchow, AIA (1922–1991), are catalogued and held at the Denver Public Library.

14. Halprin Archives, box 014 B159, folder 7023A, "Skyline Park, Denver Supervision." Correspondence of December 1971 conveys the Halprin firm's consulting relationship with Rogers/Nagel/Langhart Architects and Engineers, on the Mountain Bell Telephone Company office building. See letter from Richard Vignolo, Lawrence Halprin & Associates, to Mr. John Rogers, Rogers/Nagel/Langhart Architects and Engineers, December 17, 1971, as agreement for services proposed; and the reply from John Rogers to Richard Vignolo, December 23, 1971.

15. Halprin Archives, box 014 B159, Folder: "Denver: Towersquare" and flat drawings, 014 II A225. Lawrence Halprin & Associates, "Towersquare" Design Proposal (ca. 1972–75).

16. Halprin Archives, box files, 014.I.A.4677. Loose notes, design note dated May 19, [1970?], by Junji Shirai with a few added notes in another, unknown, hand.

17. Ibid., Loose notes dated May 19 and June 5.

18. Ibid.

19. Halprin Archives, 014.I.A.4683. Documents and notes detailing load requirements for the redeveloper of site in DURA agreement.

20. Kenneth R. Wright, "Civil Engineering, Legal, and Political Collaboration: Solving Denver's Drainage Infrastructure Dilemma," *Leadership Management for Engineering* 8/4 (October 2008): 301–05. Wright Water Engineers, a Denver-based firm, shared their archives for the Skyline Renewal Area projects.

21. Halprin Archives, 014.I.A.4683. Letter from George Hoover, W. C. Muchow Associates, Architects, Denver, Colorado to Satoru Nishita, Lawrence Halprin & Associates, San Francisco, October 14, 1970. The file also contains hand written calculations and diagrams by Lawrence Halprin & Associates showing how this will be accomplished across the block's 100-inches-by-400-feet drainage area.

22. Halprin Archives, 014.I.A.4683. Letter from Patricia Flood, P. E., Wright Water Engineers, to Tom Nelson, Chief Stormwater Planning Engineer, City and County of Denver, April 14, 1997. The study was requested at an early stage in considerations for the redesign process for Skyline Park.

23. Ben Urbonas, "Two Decades Of Stormwater Management Evolution," Presented at the Symposium on Urban Drainage, Belo Horizonte, Brazil, November 1999, http://www.udfcd.org/downloads/pdf/tech_papers/20yrs%20Stormwater%20Managemet%20Evolution%201999.pdf.

24. William DeGroot, L. Scott Tucker, and Mark R. Hunter, "Multiple Use Concepts in Floodplain Management," *Flood Hazard News–Supplement*, Vol. 15 (December 1985): 2. http://www.udfcd.org/downloads/pdf/fhn/fhn85_1.pdf.

25. Denver Urban Renewal Authority (DURA), *Skyline/Denver* (Denver: DURA, 1983), 2.

Chapter 4: Materials: Brick, Concrete, Trees

1. The brick pavers were manufactured locally at the Robinson Brick Company; they measured 4 by 8 by 1.5 inches and were a russet or rusty red color. The final installation eschewed any distinctive pattern in favor of a uniform field of brick laid in a traditional running bond pattern. See correspondence about paver materials and brick selection between Halprin's office and DURA: Memorandum to Bill Sterling, from Wayne Hecht, Office of Lawrence Halprin & Associates/DURA, October 26, 1970. Halprin Archives, box 150, file 014.I.A.4681.

2. Lawrence Halprin & Associates. *Design Specifications for Skyline Park*, 3 vols. San Francisco: Lawrence Halprin & Associates for the City and County of Denver, 1973; 1976.

3. "Thirsty People Pleasers–Haws Drinking Faucet Co., Berkeley, CA," *Landscape Architecture* 56/3 (April 1972): 192.

4. Halprin Archives, flat folder, file # 014 II. "Lighting Study over General Layout of Park–Block 18".

5. See HALS CO-01 sheets 6 and 8, and Field Notes for more information on planting. "Historic American Landscapes Survey (HALS): Skyline Park," History Colorado, Office of Archaeology and Historic Preservation, # 43028. Also available at: HALS CO-01 "Skyline Park," Library of Congress, Prints and Photographs Division, http://loc.gov/pictures/item/CO0917.

Chapter 5: Water: The Signature Fountains

1. Halprin, *Cities*, 158.

2. Ibid.

3. For more information on the contract and working agreement between Halprin's office and Herb Goldman as well as more on Richard (Dick) Chaix's involvement as the fountain

engineer, see: Halprin Archives, "Fountain on Block 18," box 150, folder [file] 014.I.A.4682 and box 159, folder 4920. Halprin worked with Chaix for over twenty-five years on various projects. Chaix began his career focus on fountain design as early as 1964 while working for Beamer Wilkinson in California. He went on to become one of the leading practitioners in this area of landscape design. He was a founding partner in 1981 of CMS Fountain Consultants. Founded in California, the firm now has offices in Santa Cruz and New York.

4. See "Plan and elevation—Fountain on block 18, Skyline Park. Scale ¼" = 1'-0" Showing Weight distribution and Gunite calculations tabulated," Halprin Archives, flat drawings, folder 014 II A255.

5. "DURA Awards Park Contract," *The Sentry*, February 8, 1972.

6. Junji Shirai, e-mail message to author, May 26, 2011.

7. Halprin, *Cities*, 211.

Chapter 6: Skyline Park's Life

1. DURA, *Skyline/Denver*, 19.

2. For example, a 1991 promotional poster urged visitors to "Come beat the heat in the shade" and listen to a series of eight lunchtime concerts in July and August; the season was produced by Skyline Talent and Production and sponsored by Denver National Bank Plaza and Metropolitan Life Insurance Company. Poster property of the author.

3. Some of this material has previously been published: Ann Komara, "Skyline Park 1973–2003," in *Conference Proceedings of the VIIIth International DOCOMOMO Conference (2004) Import-Export: Postwar Modernism in an Expanding World, 1945–1975*, eds., Theodore Prudon and Hélène Lipstadt (New York: DOCOMOMO US, 2008), 445–52.

4. I. M. Pei & Partners, The Transitway/Mall–A Transportation Project in the Central Business District of Metropolitan Denver, prepared for the Regional Transportation District, Denver, Colorado (1977), 4. The project team included Phillip E. Flores Associates, Denver (landscape consultant); Hanna/Olin, Philadelphia (environmental consultant); KKBNA, Denver (utility engineering consultant); Howard Brandston, Lighting Design, New York (lighting consultant); John O. Meadows Associates, New York (cost estimator); and Page, Arbitrio & Resen, New York (graphics consultant).

5. Halprin, *Cities*, 216.

6. The city and county of Denver maintenance crew in charge of the Skyline Park fountains ran a final test of this particular fountain in May 2003. The maintenance crew concluded, "Fountain 1 was fully operative." The author was present for this test. All 2003-era documentation field photographs showing water flowing in the first fountain were taken the morning of this test, as well as

the photographs of the interior pump room and mechanisms.

7. This phrase came into common reference through Jane Jacobs's *The Death and Life of Great American Cities*. It has also been tendered in discussions about urban spaces in the era after William Whyte's influential work *The Social Life of Small Urban Spaces* (Washington, D.C.: The Conservation Foundation, 1980).

8. The appellation "mall rat" was taken on by these young people with pride, though others used it pejoratively. During the interview, the teen noted that she had "grown up with the park." Interview given anonymously, June 6, 2002. See also: "Street Kids: Homeless youths fast becoming thorn in side of mall retailers," *Denver Post*, October (n.d), 1997; 20–21A; "The Street Life," Denver Post, Sunday, November 2, 1997, 20–21A.

9. Whyte, *The Social Life of Small Urban Spaces*, 60–63.

10. One alternative proposed for the redesign, an option sanctioned by Halprin during the Take Part workshop discussed later in this chapter, created openings through the berms along Arapahoe Street, creating more fluid connections between the park and the street.

11. "A park for people, not architects," commentary, *Rocky Mountain News*, Thursday, September 5, 2002: 44A.

12. Design Workshop, *Skyline Park Master Plan, Denver, Colorado* (Denver: Design Workshop, September 1997); Urban Strategies/Greenberg Consultants, *Skyline Park Revitalization Initiative*, prepared for the city and county of Denver and the DDP (Toronto: April 2001).

13. Michael Paglia, "Sunset for Skyline–Denver's masterful modernist park is being destroyed," *Westword*, May 15–21, 2003: 56; Trent Siebert, "Green to replace concrete at new Skyline Park," *Denver Post*, n.d. [2002]: 1B; 5B.

14. The "Request for Proposal" booklets, with a nearly complete collection of the competition entries, held by the author courtesy of Gene Bressler, a member of the selection committee, offer a whole story unto themselves. They show an extraordinary range in sensitivity regarding the Halprin original, as well as various proposals and visions for the new Skyline Park.

15. Interview materials from Gene Bressler, member of the Skyline Park selection committee; now held by Ann Komara.

16. Friends of Skyline Park, headed by Connie Wanke, ASLA. Wanke wrote several essays urging preservation of the park for the Cultural Landscape Foundation, including "How Soon We Forget: Skyline Park," June 6, 2002, http://tclf.org/print/2141; and "Skyline Park Design Threatened by Renovation," September 15, 2002, http://tclf.org/print/2139.

17. Lawrence Halprin et al., *Report: One Day Skyline Park Workshop* (San Francisco: The Office of Lawrence Halprin, May 31, 2002), 2.

18. Halprin, *Cities*, 218.

19. Lawrence Halprin, "Preserving the Designed Landscape," *Preserving Modern Landscape Architecture II*–Making Postwar Landscape Visible, editors Charles Birnbaum, Jane Brown Gillette and Nancy Slade (Washington, D.C.: Spacemaker Press, 2004): 39–41.

20. J. William Thompson, "When Is It Okay to Gut an Iconic Landscape?" *ASLA Land Matters*, LAND Online, April 18, 2005 (accessed June 2011), http://landarchives.asla.org/landsearch/archive/2005/0418/landmatters.html.

21. Mary Voelz Chandler, "High Plains Burial," *Landscape Architecture* 94/11 (November 2004): 80–93.

Chapter 7: Documentation of the Site for the Historic American Landscapes Survey

1. The project liaison at the National Park Service was Tom Keohan, historical architect, National Park Service, Intermountain Region. For further details on the documentation process see: Ann Komara, "Recording a Mid-Century Modern Landscape in Denver, Colorado," *CRM: The Journal of Heritage Stewardship*, 3/2 (Summer 2006): 94–98. Under Komara's direction, the following University of Colorado Denver students carried out fieldwork: Manish Chalana, Yi-Ping Fang, Kristen George, Arina Habich, Simone Howell, Erik Husman, Casey Martin, Carol McClanahan, Joey Noobanjong, Leanne Vielehr, Pearl Wang, Susan Whitacre, and Eugene Yehyen Chun. The drawings were produced under Komara's direction and prepared by five students: Jon D. Hunt, Zachary Peterson, E. Max Reiner, Mark Sullivan, and Sebastian Wielogorski. Research assistants for HALS were Jon D. Hunt, Carol Slocum, and Christine Taniguchi.

2. Estella Cole, historic preservation specialist, State Historical Fund/History Colorado, was the project manager responsible for the Skyline Park Emergency Documentation Grant #03-0E-005; the Skyline Park HALS Documentation Grant #04-M1-015; and Grant #08-01-051 to write and distribute this book. The documentation is on file at History Colorado. reference # 43028.

3. The total set of construction drawings for all blocks comprised a massive set, about fourteen sheets for each block. The dimensions of the blocks—long and thin, measuring approximately 110 feet across by 420 feet in length—lead to an atypical drawing size: 40 by 48 inches.

4. For more information on this documentation process, refer to Komara, "Recording a Mid-Century Modern Landscape in Denver, Colorado."

5. These documents were on file in the Department of Parks and Recreation, City and County of Denver. The team used scanned reproductions for the field work.

6. See Komara, "Recording a Mid-Century Modern Landscape."

7. The Skyline Park HALS submission contains eleven sheets of drawings, which include a cover sheet that located the park and summarized its history and significance; the rendered plan and section of the three blocks, with fountains, walls, plantings, and other features; and sheets of details as found at the time of documentation. For their dedicated work on the Skyline Park HALS, Mullins and Komara received the Colorado Historical Society's 2007 Stephen Hart Award for Excellence in Preservation.

8. Gifford Ewing, a professional photographer located in Denver, Colorado, shot and printed the HALS archival photographs and prepared the associated submittals of negatives, photo location map, and descriptions of the images. He shot a separate portfolio of Skyline Park images while completing the HALS photography.

9. HALS-CO-01, Skyline Park.

10. Videotaped and edited by Eric Altman of Q + A Films, Denver, Colorado. May 2003.

11. Mary V. Chandler, "Let's be upfront about new faces we anticipate for our public places," *Rocky Mountain News*, Saturday, February 18, 2006: 4D.

12. Letter from Stephen Bruce Gale, architect, to Mark Gelernter, dean of the College of Architecture and Planning, February 27, 2006.

13. Lawrence Halprin, "Some thoughts on Skyline Park, Denver," memorandum to Connie Wanke, Friends of Skyline Park, May 16, 2002.

Selected Bibliography

American Society of Landscape Architects. "ASLA Medals and Firm Awards." ASLA News. May 14, 2003. http://www.asla.org/newslistingdetails.aspx?id=9124&terms=halprin.

American Society of Landscape Architects. "ASLA Leaders Express: Leadership and Governance. Halprin Receives Michelangelo Award." ASLA. March 30, 2005. http://www.asla.org/ContentDetail.aspx?id=5664&RMenuId=8&PageTitle=Leadership.

ArchINFORM. "Lawrence Halprin." 2005. http://eng.archinform.net/arch/6621.htm.

Baume, Polivnick, Hatami. Urban Design and Development Study Denver Skyline Renewal Area, Project COLO. No. R-15. Denver, 1967.

Chandler, Mary V. "High Plains Burial." Landscape Architecture 94, no. 11 (November 2004): 80–93.

Church, Thomas D. Gardens Are for People; How to Plan for Outdoor Living. New York: Reinhold, 1955.

Church, Thomas D. and Lawrence Halprin. "Backyard Gardens." House Beautiful (1947): np.

DeGroot, William, L. Scott Tucker, and Mark R. Hunter. "Multiple Use Concepts in Floodplain Management." Flood Hazard News 15 (December 1985): 2. http://www.udfcd.org/downloads/pdf/fhn/fhn85_1.pdf.

Design Workshop. Skyline Park Master Plan, Denver, Colorado. Denver: Parks and Recreation Department/Design Workshop, 1998.

"Denver Skyline." HUD Challenge, April 1972, 27–30.

Denver Urban Renewal Authority (DURA. Skyline Denver. Denver: Denver Urban Renewal Authority, 1983.

"DURA Awards Park Contract." The Sentry (February 1972): 8.

Forgey, Benjamin. "Lawrence Halprin: Maker of Places And Living Spaces–The Landscapes That He Creates Are Based on a Combination of Science, Ecology, and All-Encompassing Humanity." Smithsonian 19, no. 9 (December 1988): 160–70.

Foster, Paul and Barbara Gibson. Denver's Skyline Park: A History. Denver: City and County of Denver, 2000.

Goldstein, Eric L. "Rose Luria Halprin, 1896–1987." Jewish Women: A Comprehensive Historical Encyclopedia. http://jwa.org/encyclopedia/article/halprin-rose-luria.

Halprin, Anna. Moving Toward Life: Five Decades of Transformational Dance. Ed. Rachel Kaplan. Hanover, NH: University Press of New England/Wesleyan University Press, 1995.

Halprin, Lawrence. A Life Spent Changing Places. Philadelphia: University of Pennsylvania Press, 2011.

_____. Cities. New York: Reinhold, 1963.

_____. The Franklin Delano Roosevelt Memorial. San Francisco: Chronicle Books, 1997.

_____. Le Pink Grapefruit, Film. Produced by Sue Yung Li Ikeda. San Francisco: RoundHouse, Phoenix Films, 1976.

_____. Notebooks, 1959–1971. Cambridge, MA: MIT Press, 1972.

_____. The RSVP Cycles. New York: George Braziller, 1969.

_____. "The Collective Perception of Cities." In Urban Open Spaces, ed. Lisa Taylor, 4–6. New York: Rizzoli, 1981.

_____. "The Choreography of Gardens." Impulse (1949): 31–34.

_____. "My Design Process." In Process Architecture No. 4: Lawrence Halprin, ed. Ching-Yu Chang, 10–14. Tokyo: Process Architecture Publishing, 1978.

Ching-Yu Chang, ed. Process Architecture No. 4: Lawrence Halprin. Tokyo: Process Architecture Publishing, 1978.

_____. "Preserving The Designed Landscape." In Preserving Modern Landscape Architecture II–Making Postwar Landscape Visible, eds. Charles Birnbaum, Jane Brown Gillette and Nancy Slade, 38–41. Washington, D.C.: Spacemaker Press, 2004.

Halprin, Lawrence and Anna Halprin. How Sweet It Is, Film. Directed by Lawrence Halprin. San Francisco: RoundHouse, 1976.

Halprin, Lawrence et al. Report: One Day Skyline Park Workshop. San Francisco: The Office of Lawrence Halprin, May 31, 2002.

Hatami, Marvin, and Floyd Tanaka. Feasibility Study for Skyline Park and Convention Centers Parking Structures (Skyline Urban Renewal Project, Colorado No. R-15). Denver: Denver Urban Renewal Authority, 1969.

_____. Urban Design and Development Study. Vol. 1: Urban Design Concept, Vol. 2: Implementation Standards and Criteria. Denver: Denver Urban Renewal Authority, 1970.

Hirsch, Alison Bick. Lawrence Halprin: Choreographing Urban Experience. PhD diss., University of Pennsylvania, 2008.

I. M. Pei & Partners. The Transitway/Mall: A Transportation Project in the Central Business District of Metropolitan Denver. Denver: Regional Transportation District (RTD), 1977.

Jacobs, Jane. *The Death and Life of Great American Cities*. New York: Random House, 1961.

Johnson, Charlie H, Jr. *The Daniels and Fisher Tower: A Presence of the Past.* Denver: Tower Press, 1977.

Johnson, Mark. "Skyline Park: Preservation Ethics and Public Space." In *Preserving Modern Landscape Architecture II—Making Postwar Landscape Visible*, eds. Charles Birnbaum, Jane Brown Gillette, and Nancy Slade, 42–49. Washington, D.C.: Spacemaker Press, 2004.

Komara, Ann. "Recording a Mid-Century Modern Landscape in Denver, Colorado." *CRM: The Journal of Heritage Stewardship* 3, no. 2 (Summer 2006): 94–98.

____. "Skyline Park 1973–2003." In *Conference Proceedings of the VIIIth International DOCOMOMO Conference (2004) Import-Export: Postwar Modernism in an Expanding World, 1945–1975*, eds, Theodore Prudon and Hélène Lipstadt, 445–52. New York: DOCOMOMO US, 2008.

Kupper, Eugene. "Review Symposium: The RSVP Cycles...." *Urban Affairs Review* 6 (1971): 495.

Lawrence Halprin & Associates. *Design Specifications for Skyline Park*, 3 vols. San Francisco: Lawrence Halprin & Associates for the City and County of Denver, 1973; 1976.

Lawrence Halprin & Associates. "Firm Profile Insert." *Engineering News-Record*. November 7, 1968.

Leslie, Jacques. "Profile of Lawrence Halprin." 1996/2001. http://www.well.com/user/jacques/lawrencehalprin.html (site discontinued).

Lindgren, Nilo. "Riding a Revolution, 1_1971: A Radical Experiment in Reorganization: 'A Spectacular and Poignant Attempt at Management Reform' within Lawrence Halprin and Associates." *Landscape Architecture* 64, no. 3 (April 1974): 133–39; 190–91.

____. "Riding a Revolution, 2_1973: Halprin Revisited in 1973; Still Changing 'To Stay Alive.'" *Landscape Architecture* 64, no. 3 (April 1974): 140–47.

Martin, Douglas. "Lawrence Halprin, Landscape Architect, Dies at 93." *New York Times*, October 28, 2009. http://www.nytimes.com/2009/10/28/arts/design/28halprin.html.

McEnroe, Donna. *Denver Renewed—A History of the Denver Urban Renewal Authority*. Denver: The Denver Foundation and Alex B. Holland Memorial Fund, 1992.

Mullins, M. Ann. "Remembering Denver's Skyline Park." *Historic Preservation PPN Newsletter, HALS Supplement* (Summer 2006): 3–5.

Neall, Lynn Creighton, ed. *Lawrence Halprin: Changing Places*. San Francisco: San Francisco Museum of Modern Art, 1986.

Paglia, Michael. "Sunset for Skyline: Denver's Masterful Modernist Park Is Being Destroyed." *Westword*, May 15–21, 2003, 56.

Real Estate Research Corporation, Abbott L. Nelson and Robert S. DeVoy. *Preliminary Economic and Marketability Analysis Phase 1 of Land Utilization and Marketability Study Skyline Urban Renewal Project, Project No. Colo. R-15, Denver, Colorado*. Chicago: RERC, Prepared for Denver Urban Renewal Authority, September 1965.

Siebert, Trent. "Green to replace concrete at new Skyline Park." *Denver Post*, n.d. (2002): 1B; 5B.

"Thirsty People Pleasers: Haws Drinking Faucet Co., Berkeley, CA." *Landscape Architecture* 56, no. 3 (April 1972): 192.

Thompson, William. "Master of Collaboration." *Landscape Architecture* 82, no. 7 (July 1992): 60–69.

Thompson, J. William. "When Is It Okay to Gut an Iconic Landscape?" *ASLA Land Matters*, LAND Online. April 18, 2005. http://landarchives.asla.org/landsearch/archive/2005/0418/landmatters.html.

Thompson, J. William. "From Landscape Architecture, Lawrence Halprin, FASLA, Is the First Winner of the Michelangelo Award, Given This Year by the Construction Specifications Institute." *ASLA Land Matters*. LAND Online. April 4, 2005. http://landarchives.asla.org/landsearch/archive/2005/0404/landmatters.html.

Treib, Marc, ed. *Modern Landscape Architecture: A Critical Review*. Cambridge: MIT Press, 1993.

Urban Strategies/Greenberg Consultants. *Skyline Park Revitalization Initiative*. Prepared for the City and County of Denver and the Downtown Denver Partnership. Toronto: April 2001.

Urbonas, Ben. "Two Decades of Stormwater Management Evolution." Paper presented at the Symposium on Urban Drainage, Belo Horizonte, Brazil, November 1999. http://www.udfcd.org/downloads/pdf/tech_papers/20yrs%20Stormwater%20Managemet%20Evolution%201999.pdf.

Wanke, Connie. "How Soon We Forget: Skyline Park." The Cultural Landscape Foundation. June 6, 2002. http://tclf.org/print/2141.

____. "Skyline Park Design Threatened by Renovation." The Cultural Landscape Foundation. September 15, 2002. http://tclf.org/print/2139.

Whyte, William Hollingsworth. *The Social Life of Small Urban Spaces*. Washington, D.C.: Conservation Foundation, 1980.

Wilson, William H. *The City Beautiful Movement*. Baltimore: Johns Hopkins University Press, 1989,

Wright, Kenneth R. "Civil Engineering, Legal, and Political Collaboration: Solving Denver's Drainage Infrastructure Dilemma." *Leadership Management for Engineering* 8, no. 4 (October 2008): 301–305.

Archives

The Lawrence Halprin Collection, the Architectural Archives, the University of Pennsylvania, Philadelphia, PA.

Wright Water Engineers Office Archives. Wright Water Engineers, Denver, CO.

Image Credits

Fig. 1: Drawn by Cynthia Guajardo
Fig. 2, 3, 5, 88: Courtesy Charles A. Birnbaum
Fig. 4, 10, 74, 86, 93: Image photographed by and courtesy of Gifford Ewing
Fig. 6, 7: Courtesy of Lawrence Halprin and The Cultural Landscape Foundation
Fig. 8: Courtesy of Dee Mullen
Fig. 9: *From The RSVP Cycles: Creative Processes in the Human Environment,* George Braziller, 1970.
Fig. 11: Image courtesy of Denver Public Library, Western History Collection (Z-6614)
Fig. 12: Courtesy of Denver Urban Renewal Authority
Fig. 13: Illustration taken from a document by the design team of Baume, Polivnick, Hatami
Fig. 14: Baume, Polivnick, Hatami (1967)
Fig. 15: Courtesy of Marvin Hatami
Fig. 16, 17, 26: Courtesy of George Hoover
Fig. 18: Courtesy of the Lawrence Halprin Collection, Architectural Archives, University of Pennsylvania,
    [Box 014.I.A.4680]
Fig. 19, 34, 35, 38, 39, 40, 41, 44, 45, 48, 49, 50, 51, 61, 62, 63, 66, 78, 89, 90:
    Courtesy of Ann Komara
Fig. 20: Courtesy of the Denver Art Museum
Fig. 21, 22, 25, 27, 29, 31, 32, 36, 37, 52, 53, 54, 56, 57, 60, 67, 68, 69, 70, 71: Courtesy of the Lawrence
    Halprin Collection, Architectural Archives, University of Pennsylvania, [Flat Files 014.II.A.255]
Fig. 23: Courtesy of the Lawrence Halprin Collection, Architectural Archives, University of Pennsylvania,
    [014.I.A.4920-.4921]
Fig. 24, 28, 30, 33, 42, 43, 46, 47, 58, 59, 64: Courtesy of the Lawrence Halprin Collection, Architectural
    Archives, University of Pennsylvania, [014.A.4677]
Fig. 54, 72: Lawrence Halprin & Associates, for the city and county of Denver (public records)
Fig. 55, 83, 85, 88, 95: Courtesy of Charles Birnbaum and The Cultural Landscape Foundation
Fig. 65: Courtesy of Cassidy Turley, Fuller Real Estate, Denver.
Fig. 73, 80: Photograph by Manish Chalana, HALS UCD Field Team
Fig. 75, 76: Architectural Archives, University of Pennsylvania, [014.II.A.256]
Fig. 77, 79, 81, 82, 87: Photograph by the HALS UCD Field Studies Team, May 2003
Fig. 91, 94: Drawn by Sebastian Wielogorski, University of Colorado Denver Documentation Team, 2005
Fig. 92: Photograph by Emily McMakin for the College of Architecture and Planning, University of Colorado